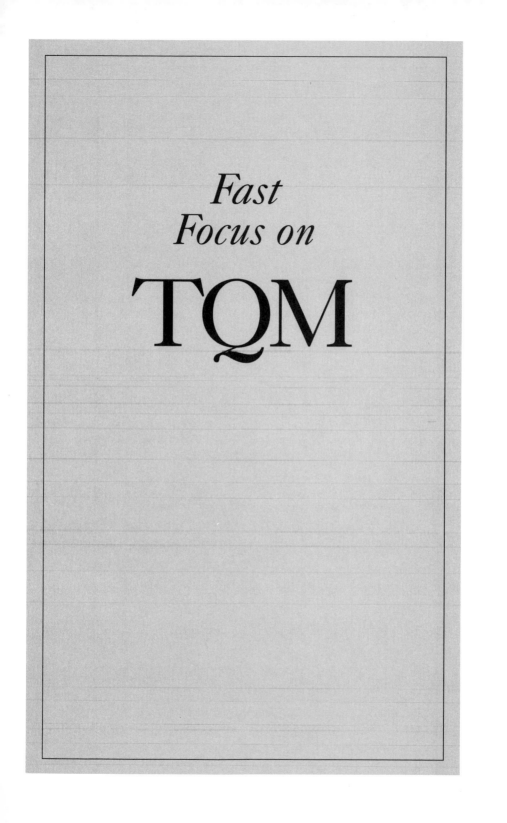

*Fast
Focus on*

TQM

Derm Barrett

Fast Focus on

a concise guide to companywide learning

Publisher's Message by Norman Bodek

Productivity Press

Portland, Oregon

Originally published as *Fast Focus: A Manager's Look at TQM Terms and Topics,* published by MCL Publications, Canada, 1990.

Productivity Press
P.O. Box 13390
Portland OR 97213-0390
United States of America
Telephone: 503-235-0600
Telefax: 503-235-0909

ISBN: 1-56327-049-8

Book and cover design by Bill Stanton
Interior design and typesetting by Frank Loose Design
Illustrations by Hannah Bonner
Printed and bound by Edwards Brothers
Printed in the United States of America

Library of Congress Cataloging-in-Publication Data

Barrett, Derm
    Fast focus on TQM : a concise guide to companywide learning / by Derm Barrett ; publisher's message by Norman Bodek.
      p. cm.
    Rev. ed. of: Fast focus : a manager's look at TQM terms and topics. Canada : MCL Publications, 1990.
     ISBN 1-56327-049-8
     1. Total quality management—Dictionaries. I. Barrett, Derm. Fast focus. II. Title.
HD62.15.B368 1994
658.5'62—dc20   93-50864
                                                CIP

98 97 96 95 94   10 9 8 7 6 5 4 3 2 1

Publisher's Message

Tqm is not a tool to be implemented," says Derm Barrett, author of *Fast Focus on TQM: A Concise Guide to Companywide Learning*, "Tqm is a state of mind."

Tqm in western organizations has had varying degrees of success. Recently, several business journals have reported that the "Tqm fad" is fading. This has been countered by numerous authors of some insight who clarify that Tqm cannot succeed if it is perceived as a quick-fix solution. Tqm must be seen rather as a far-reaching approach. It creates company structures that not only withstand but may thrive on the competitive forces and market fluctuations that characterize the late 20th century. The customer-oriented company will continue to grow simply because the whole intent and structure of the organization is *designed* to change as the customer changes.

Tqm "fails" when the intent as well as the means are not understood. The tendency of western managers is to demand instant (quarterly or at the most yearly) results from implementing a new management method, whether on the shop floor, in the business office, or in executive planning processes. They want innovation, but they *need* bottomline results. Barrett says the problem occurs when managers try to implement a tool or method rather than learn what is required to adopt a whole new approach to doing business. This can't happen in a quarter or even a year. Realistic short term goals must be set to build momentum for the major redesign underway. Such adoption requires, first and foremost, a change of mind-set — usually a manager's own mind-set.

Organized in an alphabetical arrangement of ideas and terms, *Fast Focus* sheds a bright light on the nature of this new mind-set. Barrett explores TQM's purpose, requisite management styles, foundational themes such as systems thinking and creativity, as well as the key terms and methods involved in TQM adoption. Barrett, with a PhD from MIT and a consulting practice based in Canada for many years, has successfully helped many organizations to discover the excitement of TQM. The many tools and statistical measures that companies often find daunting in the early stages of TQM adoption here become backdrop to more critical issues. The motivating power behind the TQM approach reveals itself through the many stories, descriptions, and discussions pursued in this compact and engaging volume.

Companies that have worked with Mr. Barrett in adopting TQM throughout their operations generally find that a copy of this book on every person's desk insures that everyone will use the same language during the transition to TQM. It allows quick reference to key ideas and terminology, and becomes the primer and guide for monitoring their own progress in the TQM adoption process.

Once your company has absorbed the value from *Fast Focus,* all the other books on TQM methods and tools will make sense. You will be able to choose what tools and methods to add to your program to enhance your effectiveness in employing the TQM approach. Without the understanding *Fast Focus* offers, TQM could continue to baffle.

It is our pleasure to offer the third edition of this treasure book of TQM ideas to our North American and European readers. We are grateful to Derm Barrett for the rights to do so and to his colleague Bill Christopher, another Productivity Press author, for his assistance in facilitating our correspondence with the author. We also offer our gratitude to all those whose excellence contributed to the beautiful result: to Karen Jones, managing editor; to Bill Stanton, book design and cover design; to Susan Swanson for production control; to Frank Loose for typesetting and page design; and to Hannah Bonner for illustrations.

Norman Bodek, Founder and CEO
Diane Asay, Acquisitions Editor

Preface

Total Quality Management has exploded so quickly in popularity and success that it has left large numbers of people asking what it's all about. The short answer is that TQM is an innovative integration of some very old and some very new management methods and concepts. When put into operation as a total system of management the results on business performance are nothing less than dramatic. But because TQM is a total system, a complex whole comprising many parts and elements, there is no "one-minute" way of understanding what it is. Its very scope and comprehensiveness make that impossible. There is no instant TQM literacy any more than there is instant computer literacy. Appreciating what TQM is takes time, but the question is whether the time can be significantly shortened. It can be. This handbook of TQM terms and topics will help you do it.

How can it do that? Well, TQM has a considerable vocabulary of ideas, terms and topics. Half the battle in learning TQM, therefore, is becoming familiar with the associated ideas and phrases and with the sometimes unusual meaning TQM gives them. After that, understanding TQM gets a lot easier. Building up your TQM knowledge vocabulary through the usual route of lectures, seminars, books, articles, and conversations takes months. This brief book provides a quicker way. It can be read through quickly in about three hours. Or browsed through from time to time, picking it up to read one or two separate topics each time.

This handbook defines common terms and topics and it explains common management phrases and their significance. The TQM vocabulary includes terms such as "benchmark," "delayering," and "empowerment," and phrases such as "quality of working life," "statistical process control," and "quality function deployment." Some everyday words take on important new meanings and interpretations with TQM. For example, in TQM a "customer" is frequently defined differently—and treated differently—than in a non-TQM business. The same is true of the words "manager" and "employee." And the word "time" will acquire a new importance to you.

The scope of the word "quality" extends considerably beyond traditional meaning. It is necessary to recognize from the first that TQM means the quality of management as much as it means improving the management of quality. In fact, TQM is about improving the nature and quality of management in your organization before improving anything else.

TQM requires us to first change our basic concepts about what management is, then to change the way in which we manage. It is truly a new management paradigm. It is part of a new mind-set that is outward-looking, future-focused, people-centered, idea-driven, innovative, change-seeking, and entrepreneurial. Management of change is the very name of the TQM game. TQM is itself a long overdue response to a host of changes in the socioeconomic environment that have been building up to their present momentum for twenty and more years.

Readers who have been around the management track more than once have to be prepared to discover that quite a few of the TQM ideas and methods fall in the category of "old wine in new bottles"; even when new words are used to describe them, vintage management ideas are going under a new label. But whether new, recent, or old, every single TQM idea and method has been developed, tested, and proven to work like gangbusters. The real power of these methods comes out when they are employed in concert as they are in TQM. TQM is a case, par excellence, of the "whole" being "more than the sum of the parts." Much more.

And new ideas are being added steadily. TQM is an organic and growing whole rather than a set of dogmas and doctrines, and the dust has not settled on it yet—hopefully it never will. Its rate of creative evolution is explosive. It takes on whole new dimensions as every month goes by.

While there are certain ideas and definitions within TQM that everyone agrees to, there are things that TQM managers, writers, and consultants disagree about. That will unavoidably be the case in this volume as well.

A number of my clients, suppliers, acquaintances, and colleagues have been generous with their help and contributions in developing this handbook and they are due recognition for whatever merit it has, but the final responsibility for any deficiencies has to be mine. This book owes much to them. I am grateful and appreciative. They include Steve Quinn of Du Pont Canada, Fred Irwin of United Technologies Carrier, Ross MacDonald of Quebec and Ontario Paper Company, Rick Davison of the Canadian Imperial Bank of Commerce, John Moffatt of Madison Chemical Industries, Jelle Hiel of Canadian National, Stephen Leahey of the Canadian Quality Management Centre, Carl Thor of the American Productivity & Quality Center, Irv DeToro of The Quality Network, Doug Snetsinger of the University of Toronto Institute for Customer-driven Quality, Brian Wallace of Ernst and Young, Belinda Li of the Ontario Court, John Vanderheyden of Resource Management Consultants, John Prior of J.P. Consultancy Inc., Alan Scharf of Scharf and Associates, and John Morrissey of M&M Consultants. I am also grateful for the editorial advice and assistance provided by Dee Kramer and by my editor, Diane Asay, at Productivity Press. In particular, Bill Christopher, president of The Management Innovations Group, a consulting consortium of which I am a member, has been an untiring mentor who has spent much time advising me and encouraging me from the very inception of this project. Finally, I want to thank my old friend Carlos Ferrari, of Grupo Norma in Madrid, who was the original cause of it all; the book began as a Spanish language publication in the form of a small handout given to a group of managers in Madrid whom

Carlos had asked me to speak to on the topic of TQM. The idea for preparing a book that was alphabetically constructed came up during a conversation that I had with Professor John Gordon of Queen's University in Kingston, Canada.

I have tried diligently to give credit for terms or ideas wherever credit is due. In some cases, though, I may have failed. If you come across such failures, please let me know and they will be corrected in the next edition.

Derm Barrett
Scarborough, Canada
December 1993

Directory of Terms and Topics

A

B

C

D

E

F

G

M

O

P

Q

R

S

T

U

V

W

Z

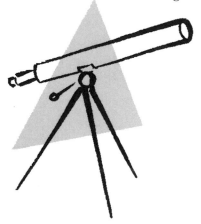

Accessing TQM

- It can take a great deal of time to know and understand enough about Total Quality Management to be able to put it successfully into operation, or to be able to judge whether it is a scheme of management that would be attractive to your organization.

- Half the battle in learning a new subject is, of course, acquiring the vocabulary and—most important—knowing in detail what the words mean.

- Understanding the vocabulary is not only a solid way to start, but also a fast way. It will save you a lot of time. When you become familiar with the vocabulary of terms and topics used in TQM you will find that you are halfway there.

- After that, it takes a two- to four-day seminar to get a truly thorough grasp.

- A great deal of further training and coaching—and thus a lot more time—will still be needed to acquire the special tools and skills and rhythm of TQM. (First you learn the words, then you learn the music.)

- However, there is no way to escape the ultimate fact that in-depth, thorough, all-out learning of TQM is a long-term process.

ACTIVITY

- Activity is a term as fundamental in TQM as the terms "power" or "current" are in the field of electricity.

- Activities are things like buying, selling, telling, phoning, writing, complaining, laughing, joking, yelling, walking, talking, designing, producing, inspecting, correcting, packing, stacking, welding, grinding, composing, computing, purchasing, planning, paying, teaching, thinking, training, advertising, assessing, etc.

- Activities are all the things that people in organizations do that result in the flow ("work flow") of products and services being produced and delivered to customers.

- In TQM, the flow of work activities is often laid out in a pictorial format, showing the various steps that take place one after the other. This format is called a "flowchart."

- The flowchart method renders work activities more easy to analyze, and to redesign and improve. It also makes it easy to attach a cost to each step and to the entire sequence.

- The diagram opposite, which flowcharts the making of a verbal presentation, illustrates how the method is used. Each step (activity) is shown as a rectangular box.

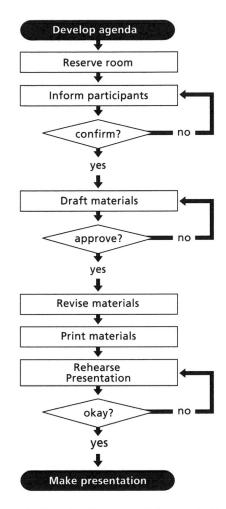

SOURCE: *CN Quality Action Team Handbook,* page 79. Reprinted with permission from CN North America, Montreal, Quebec.

- The cost of work activities—wages, salaries and benefits—approaches 90 percent of total costs in some businesses.

- TQM engages in a constant process of examining, analyzing, redesigning, and simplifying these activities in order to produce and deliver increasingly better products and services to customers at lower prices, and with less delay. (For more, see BUSINESS RE-ENGINEERING and GOALS AND OBJECTIVES.)

- At the macroeconomic level, the economic significance of work activity becomes even more vivid. Wages, salaries, and benefits constitute 80 to 85 percent of all the costs incurred in producing and delivering the nation's goods and services.

ACTIVITY BASED ACCOUNTING

- A method of accounting that establishes the true cost of a service or product by identifying the costs of some or all the work activities that go into the value-added chain, rather than by allocating overhead costs in the traditional manner.

- Also known as activity based costing (ABC).

- TQM requires a revolution to take place in the basic methods of accounting in use in the company's accounting department. The accounting department will be called upon to provide the activity-based cost data that is required in TQM decision-making.

- Many companies adopting TQM do not realize that they need new accounting methods, and as a result have more difficulty than they should in engaging in successful process improvement and business re-engineering.

- The accounting department should therefore be among the first to be asked to re-examine its methods and its role. Everyone, accountants included, have to accept the necessity of changing what they do and how they do it. (If TQM is about anything, it's about change, about radical, fundamental change in how all work is done. Accounting can be no exception. Change is the name of the TQM game.)

- To learn more about activity based accounting, read *Relevance Lost: The Rise and Fall of Management Accounting,* by H. Thomas Johnson and Robert F. Kaplan.

ADOPTING TQM EFFECTIVELY

- TQM is a comprehensive philosophy of business and management. As such, it can be adopted and put to work only in a carefully planned manner, and over an extended period of time. Full adoption may take anywhere from three years to ten, depending on where the organization is at the beginning of the process.

- Some companies are in a better position than others. For example, companies that are already practicing team management, participatory decision-making, or using extensive customer research, or employing work simplification techniques, would need less time since, without perhaps knowing it, they are already part way there.

- TQM takes time because it is so extensive. At the heart and center of TQM there lies a concern with the excellence of goods and services and the ideal of customer service and satisfaction. But the ideals and principles of quality touch upon every single thing that goes on in an enterprise. This very extensiveness of the quality principle is, of course, the reason for having the word *total* in the phrase "Total Quality Management."

- Another reason that TQM takes time is that it is not a simple set of techniques that are to be "implemented" in a linear, step-by-step manner. Beware vendors of packaged TQM "systems" who often present it in that way, as if it were a recipe for baking a cake. *It is not—repeat, not—a "program" to be implemented.* To assume that it is guarantees disappointment.

- Know that TQM is a set of values, beliefs, and attitudes that are to be adopted, absorbed, and put into practice as *a new way of organizational and business life.* TQM is a philosophy for thinking and acting effectively and creatively. TQM devotees sometimes speak of it as "getting religion," when trying to express this thought; they are also quick to point out that they do not mean by this a set of dogmas and doctrines, but a set of practical beliefs and methods that make sense.

- Only when TQM is absorbed at a way-of-life level, can it work. This is not a pious platitude, it's a tough truth.

- TQM takes time because it requires considerable training and learning. TQM uses a wide range of modern management concepts and methods, a far broader range than most managers and employees are familiar with.

- Each organization has to set a unique course into TQM and each is bound to go in a different direction. Thus each ends up with a TQM that is uniquely its own.

- Successful adoption of TQM requires:

  1. Leadership and commitment from the CEO;

  2. Strategic, visionary, and conceptual thinking ability on the part of top management;

  3. A climate of respect for the dignity and importance of the human individual and his/her creative abilities, along with convictions favorable to employee participation in decision-making, creative thinking, and self-management through empowerment;

  4. Intensive communication, training, and education;

  5. New reward and recognition systems;

  6. A support system of facilitators, guides, and trainers;

  7. The incorporation of TQM into the corporate planning and strategic management process;

  8. A fundamental revision in the principles and methods in use by the Human Resources Department and the Accounting Department (conventional HR and accounting practices as commonly used in industry and government today are often antithetical to TQM).

ALIGNMENT

- Alignment refers to the condition that exists whenever two or more people have their sights set on the same goals and objectives and share common beliefs about the best and most ethical ways of achieving them.

- There is no such thing as perfect alignment, since individuals vary in their perceptions of the same supposed goals and can never have the same beliefs about how best to achieve them.

- Nevertheless, an organization with unity of understanding about the ends to be attained and the means for attaining them will be able to focus energies and resources in a highly efficient and effective manner.

- Achieving a condition of good alignment is difficult. It can be achieved only when the organization employs a formal and explicit process of goal-setting, objectives formulation, planning and implementation that cascades downwards, upwards, and laterally from the corporate level to divisional and unit levels and back again, in a self-modifying system of feedback loops. *In TQM, the fundamental focal point of alignment is on the needs, wants, and expectations of the customer.*

- The attainment of continuous alignment, which includes ongoing realignment, requires a great deal of education and training at both a conceptual and practical level in the principles of goal-setting, planning, implementation, feedback-control, and auto-correction.

- In addition, it necessitates a great deal of rich face-to-face communication, particularly about visions and values.

- See MANAGEMENT PROCESS and MBOR—management by objectives and results—for more discussion about the principles and practices used to achieve and maintain alignment.

APOLLONIAN MANAGEMENT

- Apollonian management is a style based on data gathering, calm reason, analysis of facts, careful measurement, attention to details, minute control, sober judgment, careful thought, and prudent evaluation of costs and benefits.

- Apollo was a god of the Greeks admired for his perfect physique and balanced ability to do many things with precision, order and perfection.

- The Apollonian emphasis on doing things right—in the best way—was characteristic of the early, more technical, quantitative and numerical period of "scientific management" and "quality control," as it emerged in the manufacturing industry of the late nineteenth and early twentieth century.

- The manufacturing industry "Apollos" of this period were engineers and mathematicians with a strong bent toward measurement, regulation and control. They shared a common condemnatory attitude toward disorder, sloppiness, and waste and to the reigning system of management that permitted it.

- The Apollonian spirit of perfectionism is a very prominent part of the modern TQM movement.

- It is also somewhat suspect in the eyes of some supporters of TQM who, while equally admiring of quality and order, also place a value on spontaneity and spirit.

- For more on this point see DIONYSIAN MANAGEMENT and CREATIVITY later in the handbook.

AQL

- AQL is an acronym that stands for "acceptable quality levels."

- The idea at the time the phrase was coined referred to levels of quality below which a product or service should not fall.

- AQL is now regarded as an obsolete concept because it focuses not on being the best one could be, but on doing no more than is necessary for products and services to pass muster.

- The concept was supported by the notion—now disproved—that any and all attempts to raise quality levels above the minimum required would incur additional costs.

AUTHORITARIAN

- The authoritarian management style is the traditional command-and-control approach to quality, productivity, cost management, and all other aspects of business.

- It entails the use of external controls that are functionally exercised by specialized staff departments.

- Authoritarian management leads to the extensive use of official rules, regulations and procedures as a means of controlling work.

- It supports close supervision and/or unsolicited monitoring by a supervisor, camera, clock, or listening device to assure compliance with established procedures and regulations.

- It prefers the use of inspectors to check up on work in contrast to self-inspection by workers.

- It endorses the policy of "motivating" personnel through rewards and penalties—using the "carrot and stick" philosophy—in contrast to encouraging performance through intrinsic pride, self-motivation, and self-control.

- When practiced in a velvet-glove form, it is often referred to with the softer-sounding euphemism, "authoritative."

- Current research shows that the authoritarian style continues to be more common than TQM's participatory, self-control, self-management, and empowerment mode.

- The TQM processes depend on discarding authoritarian modes, and replacing them with employee participation and empowerment, and with a greater respect for the dignity and autonomy of the human individual.

- TQM managers believe that the authoritarian mode fails to bring about the levels of quality, productivity, and performance needed to compete in the global marketplace.

AWARDS

- An important feature of the worldwide TQM movement is that many countries have created national awards for quality management.

- The Canada Awards for Business Excellence contains a special section for quality.

- The Japanese Deming Prize, established in 1951, honors an American consultant, Dr. W. Edwards Deming. Dr. Deming has been credited by the Japanese for helping their manufacturing industries achieve levels of quality that have made them pacesetters for the world. He championed employee involvement and the use of statistical methods.

- The Baldrige Award bears the name of the late U.S. Secretary of Commerce Malcolm Baldrige, and was established in 1987 by Ronald Reagan. There are three categories: manufacturing, service, and small business. Companies are judged on seven standards of excellence: leadership, information and analysis, strategic quality planning, human resources utilization, quality assurance of products and services, quality results, and customer satisfaction.

- The European Foundation for Quality Management established a Pan-European award in 1992.

- The European Quality Award uses the criteria of customer satisfaction, people, business results, processes, leadership, resources, policy and strategy, and impact on society.

- Their model of the criteria is shown below. (Note the European emphasis on business results on the one hand, and impact on society on the other.) The diagram is adapted from the Foundation's *Annual Review*. The *Annual Review* is, as we might expect, published in several different languages.

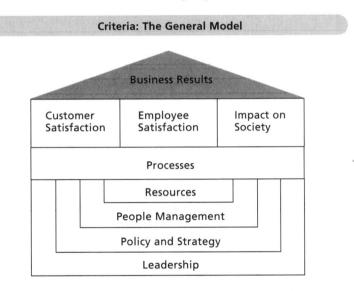

Criteria: The General Model

Business Results

Customer Satisfaction	Employee Satisfaction	Impact on Society

Processes

Resources

People Management

Policy and Strategy

Leadership

SOURCE: EFQM 1991 Annual Report, p. 9. Reproduced with the permission of the European Foundation for Quality Management.

BALDRIGE CRITERIA

- C. W. Reimann, director of the Baldrige Award, explained in a 1990 *Fortune* article the essence of what the examiners look for. Here are the eight things he cited:

    1. A plan to keep improving all operations continuously.

    2. A system for measuring these improvements accurately.

    3. A strategic plan based on benchmarks that compare the company's performance with the world's best.

    4. A close partnership with suppliers and customers that feeds information back into operations.

    5. A deep understanding of the customers so that their wants can be translated into products (and services).

    6. A long-lasting relationship with customers, going beyond the delivery of the product to include sales, service, and ease of maintenance.

    7. A focus on preventing mistakes rather than merely correcting them.

    8. A commitment to improving the quality that runs from the top of the organization to the bottom. (Main, 1990, pp. 101–116.)

- In an item that appeared in *Technology Resource* in 1992, Noel G. Thomas, former vice president responsible for quality at Dofasco, draws attention to the Baldrige criteria to warn against mistaking Quality Assurance alone for the whole of TQM. He emphasizes that TQM's success depends on the quality of the company's management process, starting with strategic planning. Thomas points out that in TQM, strategy sessions must involve major stake-holders, including the line departments.

- The seven Baldrige categories are arranged by Thomas in a flow-chart—shown below—which depicts the TQM sequence. (Flow-charts are a tool that TQM practitioners employ when they study any process—including the process of TQM itself!)

Driver	System	Progress Measure	Goal
	Strategic Planning		
Leadership ➡	Human Resources	➡ Quality Results	➡ Customer Satisfaction
	Information Systems		
	Quality Assurance		

SOURCE: Noel Thomas, "Total Quality Management (TQM) Hinges on Management's Commitment," *Technology Source* 5, no. 1:3 (1992).

BENCHMARKING

- Benchmarking is the act of finding out what the best practices and processes are in business—the best of the best, anywhere in the world—and adapting and implementing them, or even going them one better, in your own firm.

- You compare your organization and its processes, in their respective disciplines and functions, to the leaders no matter where found, and not necessarily in your own business.

- You use what you find, and adapt it creatively to your own business in order to produce breakthrough results.

- David Kearns, former CEO of Xerox, defines benchmarking as measuring yourself continuously against industry leaders and against your toughest competitors.

- Companies report large results from benchmarking. The ratio of the benefits to the costs of doing benchmarking studies is usually greater than five to one. Hard to beat!

- By studying the First National Bank of Chicago's electronic data-transfer techniques, Motorola was able to find ways of auditing its own books in 8000 fewer hours.

- Xerox went to L. L. Bean, one of the world's biggest and best mail-order firms, to find out how to become better at inventory and warehousing.

- Benchmarking was how Japanese typewriter manufacturers took the bar-coding technology used in the grocery industry and used it as a means to control their manufacturing processes. (Students of creativity and innovation use the term "concept displacement" to describe how these manufacturers took something from one field and applied it in another. It's a dandy way to innovate. To take another illustration, a young surgeon at Royal Victoria Hospital in Montreal developed a life-saving technique for temporarily zipping up large abdominal incisions. The idea came to him one day when he noticed a long zipper running down the front of a tailor's dummy that was standing in a store window as he happened to pass by! Voilà, the displacement of a concept. The invention has saved many lives. (I've been teaching concept displacement for years because it's an easy and clever way to come up with bright ideas no matter what it is you're working on.)

- If you're interested in the origin of words, the term *benchmarking*, according to business writer Jesse Cole, comes from land surveying, where a mark on a permanent object indicates elevation and provides a reference point.

- The diagram below shows how one TQM organization, the American Quality & Productivity Center, portrays the benchmarking process.

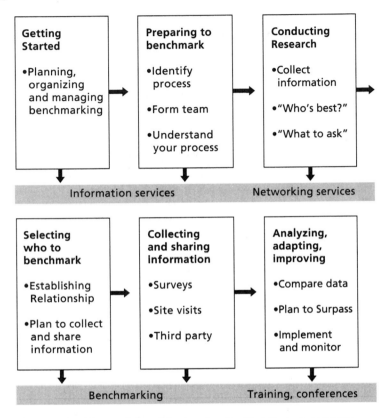

Getting Started
- Planning, organizing and managing benchmarking

Preparing to benchmark
- Identify process
- Form team
- Understand your process

Conducting Research
- Collect information
- "Who's best?"
- "What to ask"

Information services   Networking services

Selecting who to benchmark
- Establishing Relationship
- Plan to collect and share information

Collecting and sharing Information
- Surveys
- Site visits
- Third party

Analyzing, adapting, improving
- Compare data
- Plan to Surpass
- Implement and monitor

Benchmarking   Training, conferences

SOURCE: Reprinted by permission of the American Quality & Productivity Center.

- APQC operates the International Benchmarking Clearinghouse, which helps firms learn how to do benchmarking, and also helps them by providing information, newsletters, research findings, case studies, help and advice.

- Information can be obtained by faxing (713) 681-5321 in Houston, Texas.

BIG Q, LITTLE q

....

- The term *Big Q*—coined by J. Juran—means the big-picture type of quality management that strives for quality across the entire spectrum of strategic business functions—including the functions performed by top management itself. Big Q embraces leadership, strategy, management, technology, ecology, ethics, and other large issues governing corporate excellence. It is truly "total."

- *Little q* refers to the earlier, more limited—even though quite substantial—forms of quality management, wherein quality attention was centered primarily on products, customers, suppliers, services and processes, and on teamwork and employee involvement.

BREAKTHROUGH STRATEGIES

....

- Breakthrough strategies are imaginative, trail-breaking moves that set action going in a new direction, a direction that permits escape from previous constraints.

- They reshape and redefine the situation in some fundamental way.

- Breakthrough strategies do not improve a situation so much as restructure and transform it.

- When successful, they bring about large advances in a relatively short time.

- Breakthroughs are usually inspired by deep desperation, strong ambition, or some other potent stimulus to the will.

- Being new and untried—and major in their nature—they contain substantial elements of risk.

BUSINESS PARADIGMS

- Business paradigms are *frameworks* that provide different *ways of looking at* what a business is, and how it should operate in order to function best. Think of them as ideas or viewpoints.

- They are extremely important in that they are utilized as conceptual templates for shaping and forming the concrete character of an enterprise, and thereby actually making it whatever it is. They have powerfully practical effects.

- For example, Thomas Watson of IBM built that company around a specific set of paradigms, which gave it a unique and extremely powerful character. For details, the reader is referred to Watson's book, *IBM—A Business and Its Beliefs.* In this case, the paradigm he brought to bear was heavily behavioral and ethical and suffused with explicit humanistic values, apparently derived from his own political, religious and moral concepts.

- In the late eighties, additional paradigms began to be imposed on IBM with the purpose of enabling IBM to become more flexible, adaptive, innovative, and entrepreneurial; for example, the "small is better" concept of dividing the company into a number of semi-autonomous business units.

- Paradigms come in a large variety of forms and shapes. One familiar paradigm is that of *mass production,* where the idea is that a company can best survive, grow and be profitable by producing huge quantities of low cost, low price standardized goods. (Henry Ford)

- Another common paradigm is the *innovation* paradigm where the concept is to invent and market an unending stream of original, new products. (3M)

- The *selling* paradigm is another: success is viewed as attainable chiefly through aggressive selling and promotion—as we see manifested in cigarettes, soft drinks, encyclopedias, and insurance.

- The *management* paradigm—plan, organize, communicate, implement, measure, and correct—first formulated around 1900 by French industrialist Henri Fayol served to turn around GM in the 1920s and GE in the 1950s.

- The *stakeholder* paradigm replaces the traditional legal view that a company belongs only to its owners with the new legal view that other groups—called "stakeholders"—also have a legitimate stake in the business, and rights that must be protected. These other stakeholder groups include employees, managers themselves, customers, suppliers, and the community. The practical consequence—as a matter of law in some jurisdictions—is that managers are no longer legally free to make business decisions solely on the grounds of shareholder interests; they have to take the interests of the other stakeholders into account.

- The *systems* paradigm is one in which the business is deliberately engineered to function as a system of integrated and interconnected activities, all acting harmoniously together. The systems paradigm is rapidly gaining more attention. It is fundamental—indeed crucial—to TQM. It is also the basis for what is called "re-engineering the business." Leading management authorities, such as Peter Drucker, see it as the approach that will eventually govern the future of business.

- The *marketing* paradigm—also prominent in TQM—represents the belief that—to quote one of its exponents— *"the business objectives of the organization can best be achieved through the complete satisfaction of the end user—the customer."* (For a general exposition see Philip Kotler, *Marketing Management.*)

- It is certain that the 1990s will witness more business paradigm shifts than any other decade in history. TQM tries to consciously challenge, re-examine, and redefine the question, *which paradigms work best?* Year by year, it has expanded in its scope and its richness. One of TQM's important characteristics is that it goes a long way toward integrating the human, financial, and technical aspects of business.

BUSINESS PERFORMANCE

- Whenever an organization succeeds in functioning within the TQM paradigm, its performance improves *in every respect.*

- Research by A. T. Kearney, a leading TQM advisory firm, reveals that the stock prices of TQM firms during the eighties grew at a 16.9 percent compound annual rate compared with 10.9 percent for the Standard and Poor 500 during the same period.

BUSINESS RE-ENGINEERING

- A good definition of business re-engineering appeared in *Fortune* magazine: ". . . the radical redesign of business processes to achieve major gains in cost, service or time." (Stewart, 1993, p.42) It is also more simply called "re-engineering" for short.

- Re-engineering is an application of the systems and marketing paradigms described under BUSINESS PARADIGMS.

- Re-engineering is a challenging attempt at a creative retrofitting and re-creation, usually aimed at tearing apart a Rube Goldberg-like creation and substituting a more rational setup.

- Among other things, it's an exercise in hindsight—and possesses hindsight's usual crystal clarity—which will often show that:

  1. the system was never designed right in the first place,

  2. it grew ad hoc like Topsy over time,

  3. it has components that fit badly together, and

  4. it therefore came to perform its intended function poorly.

- The basic procedure in re-engineering is to rethink what the ideal or theoretically perfect design would be and then build the company (or some part of it) in that ideal image.

- The need for re-engineering is widespread. Many companies in many different industries are re-designing their businesses in radical ways, with the intent that the re-engineered business will function better. There's a sense that many companies have been jerry-built and much of the business structure of whole industries is calling for an overhaul, an updating, and modernization.

- Re-engineering a company is a bit like re-engineering an unsatisfactory house. Our house or (some of its parts) isn't performing the functions we want. It just doesn't serve our purposes well. Maybe the bathroom or the kitchen has to be torn apart and redone. But maybe the best bet is to tear the house down, hire an architect, and build a new one.

- Business re-engineering entails both analysis and design and not either alone. It takes a look at the whole business process, step by step, from the supplier end right on to the consumer end, to the point of sale and even farther, then inventively redesigns the whole works. It's a marvelous opportunity for logic and imagination to work hand in hand.

- It examines the consumer's experiences in buying and using the product or service. Then beyond that, it looks at the way in which used products are disposed of, or resold.

- There's little limit. Business re-engineering can extend still farther than that—it can examine what happens to the user, for better or for worse, as a result of using the product or service. It can go so far as to examine what happens to the quality of life of a society or nation as a consequence of the production and use of the product or service in question. Or what happens to the quality of life for people, plants, and animals on the planet as a whole, and to the air, water, and light they need.

- In sum, the product or service, as well as its production and delivery, may consequently be redesigned to better meet human needs and expectations. Any and all steps in the supplier-producer-consumer chain can also be repositioned, replaced, or redesigned. It's "value added" at every step. The outcome is a more efficient, effective, and total flow. The intention is to deliver the best quality of goods or services in the least time and at the lowest cost and to the maximum benefit of each and all the stakeholder groups.

- In the particular case of new business start-ups, the challenge is to design it (engineer it) right in the first place. When Michael Dell decided to build a computer company that would bypass wholesalers and retailers, selling directly to the end user, he engineered a business that has a unique way of functioning. Dell's success story is already a legend.

- A current example of new-business engineering along contemporary total systems lines is the huge Aikenhead hardware "warehouse" in Toronto where retail customers not only go to buy at wholesale prices but are assisted by customer service people who provide them with technical advice on their do-it-yourself home projects. The customer assistance is thorough and painstaking. Service to the customer even goes so far as to provide them with a wide array of do-it-yourself seminars.

- Another case is Price Club's huge warehouse store in Montreal; it has designed its linkage with suppliers in such a way that it can order drills on Friday from Black and Decker's Brockville plant, have them manufactured on Monday, and put them on sale in Montreal on Tuesday.

- In TQM, the goal is to create a system that is not only customer-driven but will also enlist the efforts of all the links in the value-adding chain—shareholders, managers, employees, union, community, and suppliers.

- The *total systems approach,* then, is what we can call today's methodology of business engineering and business redesign. It is a broad trend, with profound implications. It's destined to sweep through the whole of the business world. Its aim is nothing less than to "re-invent the corporation." It is the shape of things to come.

- Some firms therefore understand that the total systems approach catapults us into a new era in business management. They are actively participating in it. Others know it is happening, yet are too passive to take hold and move with it. Others are sublimely unaware of its existence.

- Today, many of the new companies being created are rationally and logically designed for optimum performance right from the start by a new breed of owner managers who know what they want, why they want it, and how to get it. When they are designed in this proactively intelligent way, their performance is so superior to older competitors that the old competitors, in order to compete, are virtually forced to re-engineer, to pull their socks up, whatever the cost and the difficulty.

- Let's put it in a nutshell. Business re-engineering appears to be something very new, but it isn't. It's a long-established discipline, and a basic part of the industrial engineering and management sciences taught in every good B school. But almost overnight the discipline has acquired a new prominence and visibility. Why? Because it possesses a unique power—the power to make a firm super-effective and super-efficient. That makes it just what we need in today's environment of fierce competitiveness when nothing less than excellence, quality, and good value for the dollar will do. Expect business re-engineering to stick around for a long time to come.

CATALYST

- A catalyst is someone who—in the Socratic tradition—does not tell and instruct others, but who, through discussion and dialogue, enables them to think, plan, work and act more effectively, and to do things more easily and expeditiously.

- Playing the role of catalyst is one of the special functions of an in-house TQM adviser.

- In general, all individuals in a TQM firm are expected to help their colleagues in this manner.

CATEGORIES OF TQM USERS

- TQM can be used anywhere: in research, in teaching, in consulting, in government, in security, in defense, in penal administration, in entertainment, in athletics, and on and on. It has no boundaries.

- The "quality of patient care" is an obvious concern of hospitals. Philip Hansen, CEO of St. Joseph's Health Centre, remarks that before TQM, patients in the emergency ward sometimes had to wait hours before receiving help. Nurses and other medical staff came up with an idea for triage and fast-tracking. Waiting time has been reduced from an average of 170 minutes to 45 minutes.

- "Quality education" is an obvious focus for schools and colleges. For example, a nation-wide student conference on the (poor) quality of teaching in universities was recently held in Canada. The quality of education can be improved by the application of TQM principles, and attempts are beginning in this direction. The University of Maryland at College Park has chosen to regard its students as customers. Under the inspired leadership of the university's president and a top-level quality council, continuous improvement programs are well underway and a number of improvements already have been brought about with great benefit to the students. (For the full story, see Kay Moore's article in *The Quality Observer*, July 1992. To purchase a copy, fax them at 703-691-9399.)

- Katherine Mangan reported in *The Chronicle of Higher Education* on some of the fascinating work done with TQM at Oregon State University in both the administrative and the classroom side of things. One professor, Eldon Olsen, had students form a TQM team to help him improve his teaching. The team surveyed students' opinions, analyzed the data, and suggested improvements.

- In June 1992, The American Association for Higher Education formed the Academic Quality Consortium to bring together academic institutions using TQM.

- TQM is moving rapidly into application in government. The popular phrase is "re-inventing government." Government is being de-bureaucratized, made more responsive to the consumers of government services, and improved in quality and productivity just as business is. Working under the leadership of Vice President Gore, the U.S. government has committed itself to a mammoth long-term program of change and improvement. The program applies the same principles and methods as those contained in TQM. Several state governments, for example Wisconsin's, have already been at it for a number of years, generating the same kind of success stories as we hear of in business. The federal government in Canada for several years now has been shifting away from the old management paradigm and into the new TQM type, also with impressive results. So have some provincial governments and some city governments.

- The fact is that it's hard to find a single institution in today's world where TQM is not moving in somewhere. The reason is that the new paradigm functions better than the old one ever did.

CAUSE AND EFFECT

- The causes of the great surge in growth of TQM are not hard to find. The basic one has been consumer dissatisfaction, verging often on anger.

- They include a need on the part of today's stressed-out consumers for products and services that are reliable and dependable.

- They include a desire to have this at a lower cost in times when purses are stretched permanently thin.

- They include increases in free trade, worldwide transport, and telecommunications facilities—globalization—which makes these consumers targets for suppliers from everywhere.

- The sequence of causes that lead to the widespread strategic adoption of TQM—with its policies of continuous improvement, and frequent innovation—is depicted in the fishbone diagram below.

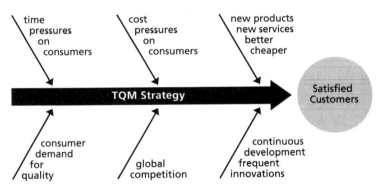

CELEBRATIONS

- TQM accomplishments are celebrated on many levels. They can be international, national, local, corporate, or divisional.

- Prizes, awards and congratulations are given in an environment of publicity, enthusiasm and high spirits. Celebrations reflect the social and emotional side of Total Quality Management— its spirited, Dionysian aspect. (See Dionysian Management.)

Champion

- A champion voluntarily takes on the responsibility for an undertaking out of a spirit of dedication and commitment. A champion will exhibit persistence, tenacity, and courage in overcoming obstacles.

- The champion's eye is always on the goal, and he or she finds a way to get there. The champion overcomes or gets around obstacles, makes things happen, and produces the desired result.

- TQM will only take root when an organization possesses a significant number of such dedicated people who have an intelligent devotion to some particular part or parts of TQM, as well as to TQM as a whole.

Change

- Change is an alteration or transformation in anything which, when positive, brings about an improvement in the nature, quality, or value of a process, a product, a person, an organization, or a business.

- Change can be incremental (a snail crossing a road) or transformational (caterpillar into butterfly). It can be slow or fast, linear or exponential, superficial or deep, gradual or abrupt, creative or destructive, desirable or undesirable, predictable or unpredictable, planned or accidental (serendipitous).

- Changes can be human, social, spiritual, mental, organizational, managerial, technological, economic, or political.

- Organizations that successfully make the transition to TQM often refer to it as a "metamorphosis," a fundamental transformation in their nature and character. Going TQM implies a decision to profoundly change the corporate culture.

- TQM organizations engage in a life of perpetual change. In a TQM organization, the triple purpose is to:

  1. survive and thrive by adapting to change;

  2. take advantage of the new opportunities provided by change; and

  3. create constructive social, economic and technological change in the marketplace through creativity and innovation.

- Everything changes, including change itself. This is what we call "hyperchange." Hyperchange exists when four kinds of change—linear, exponential, discontinuous, and random change—all exist at the same time, bringing us in touch with the volatility, turbulence, turmoil, ambiguity, and unpredictability of the world today. Expect it to increase.

- People in today's vortex of hyperchange need to support one another, keep fit, move fast, develop skills in stress management, and learn how to employ ingenuity and imagination more than was ever necessary in the past; companies need to provide their people with training in these new survival, health management, and performance abilities.

- Traditional management methods of planning and control have decreasing validity in an environment of hyperchange. Reliance must be placed more and more on the disciplines of negotiation, collaboration, compromise, enterprise, entrepreneurship, and innovation.

CLOSE TO THE CUSTOMER

- In order to be able to meet and exceed the customer's expectations, it is necessary to know the customer well. This requires a certain form of closeness, which can be brought about by direct contact and personal communication.

- Under TQM the customer is not seen as someone apart from the business—as a statistic—but as someone who is part of the business, and whose business you are part of.

- GE's relationship with its customer Praxair illustrates what mutual closeness can mean—GE has engineers stationed full-time at Praxair to help this customer increase productivity.

COMMUNICATION

- Communication occurs when people exchange thoughts, feelings, and ideas mainly through face-to-face interaction in a climate of equality, mutual trust and respect, and an atmosphere of openness, freedom and purposefulness.

- In TQM organizations, the flow of communication upwards and sideways exceeds the amount downward.

- The amount of information coming into the organization exceeds the amount going out.

COMPANY AWARDS

- Companies as well as countries and industries can and·do provide quality awards to their managers, employees, units, departments, or affiliates. For example, Banc One Corporation offers an array of awards, one of which is the chairman's "Quality of Customer Service Award" for affiliates; its objectives are to recognize quality excellence, promote greater quality awareness, and publicize effective quality strategies.

- The Baldrige-like criteria used for Banc's chairman awards are leadership, strategic quality planning, human resources utilization, information and analysis, quality assurance, and customer satisfaction. (See Arthur R. Tenner and Irving J. DeToro, *Total Quality Management*.)

CONTINUOUS IMPROVEMENT

- Improvement is one of the main anchor words and principal values in the TQM movement. It is based on the conviction that everything can become better, and its quality and value can be raised both incrementally and in quantum leaps.
- Continuous improvement requires an all-surrounding corporate climate in which there is a passionate striving for customer-oriented improvement, innovation, and progress.

CONTINUOUS INCREMENTS

- Daily improvement in small amounts carried out in every job and function in the business eventually accumulates into very large gains.
- The cumulative effect of enough small changes can sometimes be transformative in nature.
- Steady improvement can eventually transform a ho-hum product into an ultimate jewel. Look at the difference between early black-and-white TV and the modern color version.
- Or take the case of a habit of regular savings. Steady saving, carried on long enough, can turn an ordinary person, who has been living off a wage or salary, into a rich person living off dividends.

- This remarkable result of incremental change is known as Engel's Law, which states that *"quantitative change produces qualitative change."*

- The strategy of working away at incremental improvements contrasts with, but does not contradict, the alternative strategy of making quantum leaps, which requires major breakthroughs.

CONTINUOUS INNOVATION

- The word innovation comes from the Latin word nova meaning new. Francis Bacon immortalized the innovation ethic when he said: *"He that will not apply new remedies must expect new evils; for time is the greatest innovator."* This Baconian spirit of continuous innovation is a governing concept—an imperative principle—in advanced TQM.

- Many small quality improvements—which are in truth minor innovations in their own right—take the form of changes in the design of already existing products and already existing services. Others take the form of improvements in ways to produce or deliver them.

- Quality improvement can also come in bigger leaps—from new products and services that have properties and qualities not possessed by their predecessors. This breakthrough/quantum leap strategy requires more courage, more imagination, more mental gyrations, more brilliance, and more risk-taking. It is not for the faint of heart, nor for those unprepared to lose.

- The rewards from quantum leaps can be enormous. Ask Steve Jobs. Ask Jonas Salk. Some business specialists believe that the most profound improvements are those that come from creative innovation—from truly deep changes in products and services— rather than from a series of minor modifications, no matter how numerous they may be.

- For example, they might cite the quality leap that occurred when IBM came out with the Selectric typewriter, a leap that left the old type-bar models—themselves improved a dozen times over—sitting in the dust. Then came the word processor …Then came…?

- Innovative improvements, both minor and major, can be put forward by anyone from customer and supplier to worker to president. TQM companies therefore go to great pains to solicit ideas from everywhere and anywhere. It is a fact that great ideas can come from the most unexpected places and persons. The history of innovation is full of the most astonishing examples of ideas sailing in from places least expected. Edwin Land got the idea for instant photography from his small daughter's displeasure at the thought of having to wait as long as she did to see the pictures her dad was taking of her. The idea of the suspension bridge was put in the inventor's mind by his angry wife who yelled at him *"hang the bridge,"* after he had stayed up too late for too many nights trying to figure out how to bridge a high and deep chasm in a certain mountain area. Examples like the foregoing are very far from uncommon. It follows that successful innovators have to swallow their own pride and egotism and respect the universality of human inspiration. The good ones do.

Continuous Personal Improvement

- The TQM concept of continuous improvement embraces every-thing—including the personal qualities and abilities of all employees and managers.

- In TQM firms, employees set goals for self-improvement, conduct their own self-appraisal, then work out and implement personal improvement plans.

- The human craving for self-improvement has a long and respected background. It can be traced as far back as Socrates' maxim, *"know thyself,"* and to his stricture that *"the unexamined life is not worth living."*

- Self-improvement methods are described in the writings of the Stoic philosophers of Greece and in writings of Roman emperor Marcus Aurelius. (The president of one consulting firm keeps a reference copy of the *Meditations of Marcus Aurelius* on his bedside table.)

- In America, the ideal of self-improvement drew inspiration from the how-to-do-it writings of Benjamin Franklin. Since then, the self-improvement literature of North America has expanded without end.

- In turn-of-the-century France, self-improvement drew some momentum from Couism, an autosuggestion doctrine that advocated daily repetitions of the phrase, *"Every day in every way, I am getting better and better."* It also became popular for a while in the U.S. in the twenties.

- In recent times it drew sustenance from the ideas and ideals of "self-actualization" described by Abraham Maslow.

- In Japan, self-improvement has been pursued via a highly effective, two-thousand-year-old system of Buddhist exercises.

CO-PRODUCTION

- Co-production occurs when the customer participates with the producer in the design, production, assembling, or delivering of a product or a service.

- It occurs when you open that box containing parts for a child's tricycle and follow the manual on how to put them together.

- It occurs when the Mary Kay cosmetics counselor advises her client on cosmetics and how to use them, and then helps while the client applies them for the first time.

- It occurs when the accountant advises the client on several alternative ways of paying taxes, obtains information from the client, and the two decide what will be done, and which of the two will do what.

- It occurs when a consultant teaches a client enough about TQM to allow the client to discover an interest in it and then, working hand in hand with the client, helps the client get it going, and helps the client expand it, until the point comes when the client flies alone.

- It is characteristic of co-production that the client inputs information of a factual nature as well as information about the client's needs and preferences.

- It is also characteristic of co-production that the client may work alongside the provider in designing or carrying out the actual service. Sometimes the provider-designer may even have an office provided by the client, right on the client's site.

- In this format, the pair can be seen to be acting as a *single* team that is pursuing a common goal. They engage in a continuous stream of information exchange and feedback as a necessary means for planning, coordinating, and controlling the design and production process.

- This type of informational process is referred to as *cybernetic*, a term coined by the MIT scientist, Norbert Wiener. (For more details see his great paradigm-breaking book, *Cybernetics: Communication and Control in Man and Machine,* published in 1948 by Wiley.)

CORPORATE CULTURE

- TQM calls for new patterns of thinking and acting; it represents a change in traditional corporate work culture that is profound.

- A corporate culture consists of shared values, beliefs, ethical standards, habits of thought, norms and standards of behavior, and accepted patterns of work and action.

- In particular, the culture of a TQM organization must be enlivened and animated by a vision, an image, of what it wants to become, with special reference to the desired degree and scope of excellence and quality. There is an old saying, *"Where there is no vision, the people perish."* The saying applies in spades to the inspired TQM dream of the excellent enterprise.

- The TQM approach is to organize work around the natural flow of activities from department to department. This is a lateral or horizontal flow. Organizing people and their work in this new, horizontal manner, conflicts with the old vertical, command-and-control way.

- In the old vertical tradition, planning, organizing and controlling flowed downward from the top of the organization. Accountability flowed upward toward the boss. In TQM they all flow laterally toward one's colleagues, as well as to and from the boss.

- Employee empowerment—a basic in TQM—is another change in corporate culture. In the old culture employees simply obeyed and did what they were told. Even though empowerment has been part of such vanguard firms as Texas Instruments and others for many decades, it is not yet widely accepted.

- Other changes in the typical culture include emphasis on the value of entrepreneurship, enterprise, customer satisfaction, creativity and innovation.

- It is easy to see how profoundly TQM runs against the traditional grain of our whole society and its established axioms.

- When an organization embarks on TQM, it will often encounter resistance, not only from vested interests whose position and power will seem to be adversely affected but also from those who are convinced it is foolish.

- It is important to understand, have compassion for, and sympathize with, this resistance, even to the point of yielding to it temporarily. TQM would ethically contradict itself if it were to act otherwise.

- Because it tears deeply into the roots of traditional precepts for the organization of work and the conduct of organizations, TQM requires a large amount of relearning and adaptation.

- Re-learning sometimes requires a person to make a radical departure from his/her previous thinking, and to escape from fixed ideas that may have prevented them from discovering new possibilities.

  ➤ Like Columbus accepting the idea that the earth is round.

  ➤ Like doctors who had to accept the once preposterous idea that some illnesses are caused by unseen creatures called "microbes."

  ➤ Like accepting the foolish idea that a government "by the people, for the people, and of the people" could work.

  ➤ Like accepting the idea that grass roots people are responsible and intelligent.

- Fixed ideas can hold progress back for decades and even for generations. They drive our thinking, without our realizing it, almost as if they were hidden mechanical gears implanted in our skulls.

CORRECTIVE ACTION

- Taking corrective action is a basic TQM concept.

- The methodology is to monitor processes and products for errors and defects, and then to correct them in an organized way, often by corrective action teams who set out to find the root cause and do what's necessary to correct the cause and thereby prevent future defects, errors, or deficiencies. In the process, the problem-solving methods described later in this handbook will often be used.

- By failing to monitor and correct errors and defects, they compound themselves steadily until the state of neglect and sloppiness reaches unsatisfactory and intolerable levels; things go from bad to worse.

- But by diligence in monitoring and correcting, the opposite phenomenon is set in motion, and things acquire increasing quality, polish, and excellence.

- Corrective action is a process analogous to improving one's performance in golf, or writing, or music. It involves disciplined concentration and patient attention. It's how excellence is achieved in every field.

COST OF QUALITY

- Cost of quality can be divided into two categories: the cost of having good quality and the cost of having bad quality.

- The idea can be illustrated by taking the case of one industry. Charles Aubrey, vice president and chief quality officer of Banc One Corporation, describes four standard quality cost categories in financial services:

  1. *Prevention:* New product or service reviews, quality planning, quality circles, training, written procedures, quality improvement projects, etc.

2. *Appraisal:* Inspecting of incoming supplies, materials and work.

3. *Internal failure:* Downtime of equipment, rework, reprocessing of badly done work, etc.

4. *External failure:* Correcting errors made in providing a service or product, reworking it, losing customers due to bad quality. (Aubrey, 1992, p. 24. Used with permission)

- In most businesses the cost of things doing things badly rather than well, and of doing things well that need not be done at all, runs from 35 to 50 percent or more of total costs.

- Improved quality and lower costs from better processes, elimination of waste, and value-added in the customer's eyes will always result in a handsome net profit from any expenditures on quality improvement. This has been established by measurement, and by demonstrated results in firms such as IBM, Xerox, Northern Telecom, and numerous others.

- When products, services, and processes are redesigned and improved, the result is a lower cost as well as a better product or service. Those facts lend oblique credibility to Philip Crosby's cryptic catchword, *"quality is free."* This grabby catchword is not meant to imply that TQM offers a magic way to produce a Rolls-Royce for less than an Oldsmobile. Or champagne at a lower cost than *vin ordinaire.*

COURAGE

- Courage is the strength to continue to act while under threat and experiencing fear and discouragement.

- It is an attribute particularly required in the execution of breakthrough strategies, when breakthroughs are the only way to make a quality leap as against a small, slow gain.

- Courage is equally required for doing the unorthodox, out-of-the-box thinking, and for entertaining the seemingly absurd ideas that are the necessary prelude to a new strategic insight.

- Most people experience anxiety and trepidation when mentally exploring beyond the boundaries of the safe, the established, and the orthodox.

- For useful reading that convincingly explains why courage is required in order to be creative, see *The Courage to Create* by Rollo May.

CREATIVITY

- TQM is a management mode in which thinking and ideation—the production of new ideas—are the principal driving forces. It is a form of *"management by brainpower."*

- TQM is a deliberate and calculated process for mobilizing the creativity and imagination of all the people in the enterprise, including customers and suppliers.

- In the best of TQM companies everyone receives training and coaching in the use of such creative thinking techniques as brainstorming, lateral thinking, creative contradiction, paradigm shifting, morphology, synectics, and others.

- TQM recognizes that the mere day-to-day production of goods and services is a transformative process. What comes out bears no resemblance to what went in. In production, lower value inputs are changed—transmuted—into higher-value outputs. It is a magic we often fail to appreciate.

- Because of the originality involved, the design of new, different, or improved products or services stands at a very high level on the scale of human creativity. So does the design and working out of new and different production and delivery processes.

- TQM is a philosophy in which the left brain and right brain—the analytical and the creative sides of human intelligence—are both put to work. Either without the other is inadequate.

CREATIVITY QUOTES

The human infant is born curious, but their natural curiosity gradually drains away as they grow older. I consider it my job to nurture the creativity of the people I work with because at Sony we know that a terrific idea is more likely to happen in an open, free, and trusting atmosphere than where everything is calculated, every action analyzed, and every responsibility assigned by an organization chart.
AKIO MORITA, SONY

To repeat what others have said, requires education; to challenge it, requires brains.
MARY PETTIBONE POOLE

Increasingly, competition between companies and even between whole economies is taking place at the idea level—the level of creative innovation. That is, innovation not just in the technical research and development laboratories, but in all business functions.
DONALD SMALTER

To cease to think creatively is to cease to live.
BEN FRANKLIN

Imagination is more important than knowledge.
ALBERT EINSTEIN

Creativity is the struggle for improvement—the rearrangement of variables which the human can change in search for improvement.
W. W. CULP

Discovery comes as a result of a positive discontent, a constructive dissatisfaction. In fact, one may quite truthfully say that there is no discovery when one is content ...
MYRON S. ALLEN

Businessmen will have to learn to build and manage an innovative organization. They will have to learn to build and manage a human group that is capable of anticipating the new, capable of converting its vision into technology, products and process, and willing and able to accept the new.
    PETER F. DRUCKER

CREATIVITY TECHNIQUES

- In advanced forms of TQM, creative thinking has been joined to analytical thinking in a determined strategy to make broader use of human brainpower and intelligence.

- General Motors employs "Creativity Teams" to re-examine the status quo, pull the rug out from under conventional definitions, and open up fresh new possibilities.

- For several years, General Foods Canada operated an "Idea Center" where creativity teams received training in the kind of divergent and unorthodox thinking that's required. They thereupon went to work on such projects as new ways of packaging coffee, displaying cereals, or training customers. The teams met in a specially designed facility whose decor was offbeat, where relaxing music played gently in the background, and where floor-to-ceiling windows opened out on a long vista of trees and hills. Eventually creative team thinking became such a habit that a formal center was no longer necessary.

- A few of the many available creativity techniques are listed below. (For a more detailed examination of creative thinking in TQM see my article, "Driving Quality and Productivity Improvement Ahead Through Idea Generation," 2-7.1 in *Handbook for Productivity Measurement and Improvement*, edited by William F. Christopher and Carl G. Thor.

- *Bio-heuristics* (originally called "bionics") is a method for finding out solutions to business problems ranging from finance to design by finding out how organisms—ranging from bacteria to elephants—deal with problems in their own domain. The solution found in the world of organisms is minutely examined, then copied and adapted to make it workable in the business world.

> ➤ The Reebok company says that the Hexalite running-shoe technology is a conscious and deliberate use of the honeycomb, one of the strongest yet lightest shapes found in nature. Take a look at Hexalite next time you're in a shoe store. Fascinating!

> ➤ And everyone has a piece of clothing, or luggage, or something else that closes with Velcro fasteners. Velcro was a successful attempt to imitate the structure of burrs—those annoying little objects that catch onto your dog's fur. Burrs work with tiny hooks that grab, stick, and cling tenaciously. Now so does Velcro.

- *Brainstorming* is the most popular of all techniques. It uses a mental device called "suspended judgment." The purpose of suspended judgment is to turn off your "critical mind" in order to allow your "creative mind" to break through. The outflow is ordinarily prodigious and the mood hilarious at times.

> ➤ Brainstorming was invented in the early fifties by Alex Osborne, an advertising company president. His book, *Applied Imagination,* has sold millions of copies.

> ➤ Years ago, I'd scarcely heard about brainstorming when the chance came to teach it to the executives of Dyeco, a small chemical company in Ontario. Their very first attempt at brainstorming produced an idea that saved them from bankruptcy. It was an astonishing experience that neither its then president Dan Atack nor his associates and I will ever forget. A "peak experience." Thirty years later the company is still alive.

> ➤ Brainstorming takes place in two sessions. First, an "idea generation" session to produce the ideas; then, an "idea evalua-

tion" session to sift through them looking for the one that will work.

- **Concept Displacement** is the process of taking an idea invented in one field and applying it to another.

  ➤ For example, in theater people act out various roles provided by a playwright. But the concept of acting out a role has been taken from the theater and used in other settings for other purposes. Some psychotherapists ask their patients to act out various roles that will help the therapist and the patient to get a better insight into the patient's behavioral problems.

  ➤ In another and different context, industrial trainers ask sales trainees to act out an imaginary selling situation so that their sales behavior can be observed, analyzed, and improved. Video cameras are sometimes used to help the trainer and trainee look at what has happened. This use of the camera is an additional reminder that "roleplaying," as a method of industrial training, had its origin in the theater. Benchmarking, when it borrows methods from one industry to apply them uniquely in an entirely different setting, is employing concept displacement. (See BENCHMARKING.)

- **Creative Contradiction** makes use of opposites. Sometimes a creative solution can be found by doing the opposite of what seems logical or what is customary. At other times, the solution is found by combining a customary or orthodox answer with its opposite in order to create a synthesis of the two.

  ➤ People are supposed to pay the company for what they buy from it. But sometimes we see the opposite happen. My partner, Tina, got a coupon for five dollars in the mail yesterday from the Bay department store entitling her to use it to buy any object of that price. Nor are stores expected to get rich by giving their products away for nothing. But today, Tina received a letter from a grocery chain telling her to come in and pick up a free pie worth five dollars.

➤ The glass window was invented to do two contradictory things: let light in but keep air out. The shutter, in contrast, was invented to let air in but keep light out!

➤ The common rubber-tipped pencil was invented so that we could do either of two opposite things: put words on paper or take them off.

• *Lateral Thinking* is the technique of circling around the problem, turning it around, and going at it zig-zag instead of digging into it in a straightforward, logical, and linear way. Dr. Edward de Bono of Britain invented the term *lateral thinking* to describe this zig-zag process. He was the first person to recognize its existence and write about it. Dr. de Bono, in addition, has made many other contributions to the science of human thought and creativity. The term *lateral thinking* has become so popular that many people use it loosely, as if it were a synonym for all creative and inventive thought rather than for only one form of it.

• *Morphology* is a technique that utilizes a three-dimensional grid, with each dimension representing one aspect of a business design problem. Each dimension of the grid is broken down into a number of elements. Trial designs are constructed by choosing random elements from each dimension. For example, what new products could your firm make from what materials for what people?

➤ Morphology was invented by Fritz Zwicky, a brilliantly successful and totally eccentric astrophysicist who used it himself both to make scientific breakthroughs and to invent engineering devices. He said anyone who used his method would become a genius because all that his method did was to operationalize for easy use what it was that geniuses like himself did. He's certainly half right or more—I have seen managers who used it for the first time come up with creative and practical ideas that surprised them for their cleverness.

• *Paradigm shifting* consists of putting a problem into a different context in order to change how you see it, to open up new perspectives, and to examine it in a new light. For example, to look at your company within a *literary paradigm*—ask which character from Shakespeare it resembles most. Is your company an indecisive and tortured Hamlet? Or is it an Othello? Or an Ophelia? Perhaps a Richard The Third? To look at it within a *musical paradigm,* ask which department is the most musical, works to the best beat, has a good rhythm? What improvement ideas do these images of your company or its departments suggest to you? How about a *sociological paradigm?* Is it a safe haven for the "yes men" of this world? Is it an insane asylum? Is it an army of mercenary warriors? Is it an old boys' club? Is it a knitting circle? Is it a den of thieves?

- *Synectics* is a methodology that uses analogies and metaphors as some other methods also do, but it employs them through the use of an orderly, step-by-step process called an "excursion." As an added twist, it also employees an unusual type of metaphor called a "personal metaphor."

  ➤ A personal metaphor requires the idea-seeker to imagine that he or she were the object in question, to imagine that he or she were, say, a rubber ball bouncing up and down. Silly? Yes. Impractical? No. Not if you were a firm in the huge industry that invents and produces children's toys and needed some new kind of ball-based game.

  ➤ The fact is that synectics uses personal metaphors because it has been found that successfully creative people often engage in this kind of strange thinking. It turns out that it quite often produces new ideas that really work well. *Fortune* magazine once described it as "invention by the madness method." Read the book by George Prince, who invented synectics, entitled *The Practice of Creativity.* It's out of print, so you'll have to ask your librarian to get you a copy on loan.

- To really dig farther and deeper still into how to use metaphors in management read the path-breaking book, *Imaginization,* by Professor Gareth Morgan of York University. It's a remarkable book by a very imaginative thinker. Great reading, and a whole new, different, and powerful approach to organization and management. A paradigm-buster.

CULTISM

- Cultism is the tendency to define TQM as a set of fixed doctrines and methods that have arrived out of the blue, invented by genius "gurus" whose unique visions provide all the proper answers, explanations and procedures.

- In cultism, the right answers and proper explanations are to be propagated only by certified teacher-disciples and are not subject to question or debate.

- Cultism contains the danger that TQM might become for many a form of lay religion, characterized by dogmatic overtones, reverential attitudes, and the cessation of critical thought.

CULTURAL DIFFERENCES

- TQM companies that have subsidiaries in foreign countries are naturally interested in putting those subsidiaries on a TQM basis as well. And they wonder whether the culture of other countries permits TQM to be as viable there as it is at home. Despite cultural differences between one country and another, the answer is "yes."

- In Mexico TQM is thriving in Ford, in GM, in Cummins, and in GE. In some cases these subsidiaries are outdoing the parent company in quality performance and in productivity. In addition, a good number of Mexican-owned companies have adopted TQM, and have done well with it.

- One could easily cite dozens of countries and cultures where TQM flourishes. TQM strikes right into the roots of universal human nature and resonates with the nature of business, and other organizations, everywhere.

CUSTOMER

- In the vocabulary of TQM, the term *customer* covers a generous territory. It means any recipient of any product or service whatsoever, ranging from an airline passenger or a shopper in a drugstore to a student in a grade school or a patient in a hospital.

- Most TQM organizations extend the meaning of "customer" even farther. For example, a manager who receives a report from the accounting department and an employee who takes a course from the training department are both described as "customers" of the delivering department's service. They are the "internal customers."

- Thus it is concluded that "everyone has customers" and everyone is in the business of directly supplying customers with service and satisfaction. In Canada's Toronto Dominion Bank not only are regular surveys done of external customer satisfaction, but regular surveys are also done to measure the degree of satisfaction of internal customers. Branches rate the quality of the service that is provided to them by the division and corporate departments!

CUSTOMER CRUNCH

- In 1979, an international survey by Dr. A. V. Feigenbaum showed that only three or four out of ten consumers considered quality to be as important as price. In 1989, the figure had changed to nine out of ten. This rising demand, worldwide, for better quality has been a fundamental force driving TQM to its present degree of strategic importance.

- Customer dissatisfaction has come to be one of business's most serious problems, but one not always recognized. According to the U.S. Office of Consumer Affairs, the average company doesn't hear from 96 percent of those who are disgruntled. Of those whose problems with the company have been "serious," a huge 90 percent don't buy again. Moreover, the average customer who has had a problem tells nine other people about it!

- Research findings such as these have brought the business world up with a shock. They have stirred up an unprecedented wave of new attention to the customer's wants, and forced business to realize the impact that customer anger can have on their revenues. As a result, more and more companies (and public institutions) conduct regular surveys to ask customers what their feelings are, and they listen carefully to the answers.

CUSTOMER FOCUS

From a competitive point of view, quality of customer service has become the edge which one bank can have over another. Quality at the Canadian Imperial Bank of Commerce is each and every employee continuously meeting and exceeding the expectations of internal and external customers.
    RICK DAVISON, VICE PRESIDENT, SERVICE/QUALITY
    CANADIAN IMPERIAL BANK OF COMMERCE

- In a TQM company, strategic thinking directs itself unremittingly to satisfying customers, retaining customers, obtaining customers, and creating customers where none existed before.

- Under TQM the very purpose of a business enterprise's existence is to provide goods and services for consumers and users. The customer is truly king. The TQM company is devoted to the customer's interest first and foremost.

- Research conducted by the Strategic Planning Institute revealed that companies that outperform their peers in quality and customer satisfaction have profit margins of 12 percent versus 1 percent for their less customer-oriented competitors, and growth rates of 10 percent versus 0 percent.

- In TQM the quality of a product or service is defined as the extent to which it meets and exceeds the expectations and requirements of the customer.

- Quality means meeting the customer's subjective as well as objective needs and wants. It means providing the customer with a sense of pleasure, confidence, and gratification.

- The customer is considered to be an inseparable part of the business, a partner in it, a friend and colleague, an insider, and not an outsider.

- A TQM company intends—and will make sure—that a large proportion of the ideas for quality enhancing improvements and modifications will come from the customer.

- Since the customer is a part of the business, the TQM company has very organized ways to actively solicit the innovative ideas, contribution, and support of the customer.

CUSTOMER SATISFACTION

- For all practical purposes, according to the TQM philosophy, we are better off to ask the customer to define what quality means, rather than trying to define it for him or her. In fact, no other way will work. Customer *perception* is everything.

- Customers have expectations of quality which will either be (1) not met, (2) met, or (3) exceeded.

CUSTOMER SERVICE INDEX

- The customer service index is a set of criteria developed to allow customers to rate the quality of a product or service along several different appropriate dimensions.

CUSTOMER/SUPPLIER CHAIN

- The customer/supplier chain means the chain of connections that can be traced backwards from consumers to the manufacture/producer and even further back to the suppliers of raw materials and other goods and services that the provider must have in order to produce.

- The chain is illustrated in the diagram below. As a result of receiving a feedback of information and suggestions from the customer, the producer/provider's organization can change its work processes to improve them and better meet customer requirements and expectations.

- It is obvious that if a company does not actively obtain such feedback (and most do not), it is more or less shooting in the dark and can scarcely know what to do to satisfy and to keep customers. Instead of keeping the customers it has, it must always be finding new customers to replace the ones it once had but failed to satisfy.

- The supplier in this chain also needs this customer feedback information. For example, if the company sells knives that dull too quickly, the supplier—knowing of this customer dissatisfaction—might provide the company with a harder steel.

- In a TQM organization, every attempt is made to stay close to the supplier and the customer—*actively involving* them as genuine partners. In this way, all actors in the supply chain can work as a team with the one single goal of providing the customer with the ultimate in value.

- An excellent example of this kind of unified effort is Walton's, the large U.S. clothing chain. Walton's maintains several special stores in which suppliers can actually test out their products and have direct access to Walton's customers.

- Everywhere in TQM, we see this strong emphasis on groups coming closer together, sharing information, coordinating their ideas and their efforts, working hard toward process, product, and service improvement—and always basing what they do on feedback from the customer.

CUSTOMER SURVEY

- *Customer survey* here refers to any study carried out with the purpose of discovering what customers need, what they want, what they could want, what they think of what they are already getting, what ideas they would suggest for new products or services, what improvements they would like to see in existing products and services, or how they would like to see them delivered or provided.

- Surveys are carried out by means of pencil-and-paper questionnaires or by telephone or face-to-face interviews, either with customers singly or in small groups (focus groups).

- Such surveying played an important part in the development of this handbook.

CYCLE TIME

- Cycle time is the time interval that elapses between the initiation of a business action and its completion.

  - The cycle time between ordering a hamburger and receiving it at a fast-food drive-in has been reduced to a very few minutes, and the cycle time between ordering a pizza by phone and receiving it at the door has been reduced to thirty or less.

  - McDonald's has designed an oven and a recipe that delivers a very good quality pizza in four minutes versus the standard twenty—the fast-food equal of breaking the four-minute mile!

  - Frank Pasquill of Toronto, when AVP of a Canadian bank, reduced the average cycle time for design and delivery of new management courses from eighteen months to five.

  - In Winston-Salem, a quality team in Sara Lee Direct reduced the cycle time to initiate and complete the design and production of new mail-order brochures by two-thirds.

  - Du Pont in Canada has reduced the cycle time on new engineering projects by satisfyingly large amounts.

- In all these cases, the cycle time has been reduced by simplifying and redesigning work flow and work processes.

- In almost all cases, the new process not only reduces cycle time but drastically reduces the person-hours of work required to provide the output in question, whether it is a multimillion-dollar chemical plant or a hamburger in the hand.

- The shortening of cycle times is one of the most dramatic features of today's business world.

- Cycle time reduction is a necessity for several reasons:

1. Consumers are more pressed for time than ever before in human history; waiting is a luxury they can't afford.

2. Firms have to get new products and services to the market faster than ever before, initially to keep up with fast-moving competitors, and then to be ahead of them. It's called "time-based competition."

3. Reduced cycle time reduces the costs of products and services because it reduces the amount of time—the person-hours—it takes to design, produce, or deliver them. This, in turn, results in lower prices and an increase in sales.

4. In the process of working to reduce cycle time, improvements in other aspects of the quality of the product and service can be simultaneously made.

5. The net outcome of cycle time reduction is products and services that are *better, cheaper, and faster*—which is the name of today's competitive business game.

DECENTRALIZATION

- Decentralization refers to the process of placing the authority and the right to make decisions as far down in the organization as possible.

- Its purpose is to have decisions made by the people who are closest to the work and the customer—in other words, by people who are dealing with the day-to-day realities of business life, education, health care, or whatever the case may be.

- Under a policy of decentralization it is expected that the people at the top will have more time to manage the organization as a whole and to better steer its course and its strategies for survival, development, and growth.

- A policy of decentralization is easiest to implement when the nature of the business is such that it is spread out geographically, such as is the case with franchise-type operations, branch banks, local schools, and other such cases; or else when it consists of a number of business units each different in nature from the other.

- The policy of decentralization requires that each of the decentralized units be equipped with its own support functions such as accounting, personnel, etc. In addition, it will have its own sales, engineering, and manufacturing people. In other words, it's a complete business in its own right. This does not require additional employees, but means more can be done with fewer people. First of all, the often huge headquarters staffs of the centralized organizations—much of whose purpose is usually to control rather than to create—are broken up and the people moved out and down to the field. Second, the decentralized decision-makers become more energetic, motivated, and responsive to real customer and operating needs and therefore faster, more effective, and more productive. The result is that more gets done, better, and with fewer people; if this were not true, there never could be any justification for decentralization.

- An excellent illustration of the principle of decentralization and how it creates empowerment can be found in the way in which self-made U.K. billionaire Richard Branson has organized his diversified enterprise of 6000 employees. By keeping business units small—an average of only 60 persons in each—entrepreneurship, creativity, and motivation are elevated to a peak. Branson's motto is "small is beautiful."

DE-LAYERING

- Means removing excessive levels of supervision and management in order to delegate more decision-making authority to the level where the work is being done.

- In a company with a flat organization structure, information travels faster and more accurately between top and bottom, making quicker and better decisions possible.

DESIGN AND DEVELOPMENT

- In TQM, design and development is handled by multidisciplinary teams.

- The teams include customers, suppliers, R&D, manufacturing, sales, and various staff groups who all work together.

- Their single aim is to produce a product or service design that offers customers the highest quality at the lowest cost, supplied in the shortest time possible.

DIONYSIAN MANAGEMENT

- TQM organizations are Dionysian as well as Apollonian. The Dionysian approach to work, to life, and to business encourages the expression of feelings of enthusiasm, imagination, creativity, adventure, and comradeship.

- The Dionysian philosophy places high value on spirit, energy, love, will, and passion. They are perceived as the life force of the enterprise. Logic and analysis have no value without them. They are the drivers of survival, development, and success.

- The TQM organization aims at a healthy integration of Apollonian logic and Dionysian passion.

DIVISIONS

- From the perspective of today's quality revolution, organizations divide into three types:

  - ➤ Those who haven't yet decided to make a commitment to quality.

  - ➤ Those who have, but who believe that it can be done within the framework of the traditional hierarchical, command-and-control, vertically organized processes.

  - ➤ Those who believe that in order to achieve levels of quality that meet global standards—and are therefore competitive—an entirely different scheme of organization and management is necessary.

- TQM is the code word for organizations in the third category.

DRIVERS

- TQM unleashes a substantial family of driving forces. It is these forces which make it run. Some of these driving forces are:

  - ➤ teams and teamwork
  - ➤ employee empowerment
  - ➤ continuous improvement
  - ➤ constant creativity
  - ➤ management by fact
  - ➤ statistical methods
  - ➤ customer participation

> change management
> strategic entrepreneurship
> planned innovation
> cycle time reduction
> training and development

- It is the combination of all these forces acting together that produces the great power of the TQM firm.

ECOLOGY OF MANAGEMENT

- Ecology is the study of how biological and social systems, including companies, interrelate with their environment.

- The "system" in question can be a virus, a plant, an animal, a species, a family, an institution, a nation, an organization, or a corporation.

- For example, in 1953 the author of this handbook did a study of a French-Canadian labor union titled, "An Ecological Analysis of the National and Catholic Labour Union in Quebec." The relationship of organizations to their environments is now being termed *organizational ecology*. It'll be a popular buzzword throughout the nineties, and will be presented as something brand new. Guaranteed.

- The idea of the study was to show how that particular union's characteristics reflected the religious and ethnic values of its society and the theocratic and authoritarian nature of the social and political institutions that surrounded the union, impregnated it, and held it captive.

- The general idea in ecology is that everything that exists depends upon and reflects the features of its environment, and is indeed no more than a functioning part, and a reflection, of that environment.

- Living systems such as plants, animals, people, and companies are self-organizing. They modify their behavior in order to maintain their integrity and move toward their goals by drawing upon a continuous feedback of information from their environment. The information can be in many different forms: sound, heat, light, words, numbers, and others. As a result, the system—which can be anything from a caterpillar to a corporation—is in a constant process of self-correction and self-adjustment: it is self-managing. At the workplace level, this information-based, self-organizing, self-managing characteristic of systems is what makes self-managing work teams so effective.

- As everyone knows, if workers actually followed all the rules and procedures little would ever get done and much that got done would be inappropriate. Hence the immense power of "work-to-rule" protests. My colleague Bill Christopher wryly comments, *"One benefit of this self-organizing principle is that it prevents bad management from doing too much damage to the company."*

- The two things, the organism and the environment, are part of each other. The fish is in the water but the water is also in the fish, not only in its gills but as a major component of every cell. Similarly the environment of a company is just as much inside the company as it is outside the company. The people of the company, their values and attitudes, are part of the community as well as part of the company. The way things are done are largely the way things are done in that society and culture and not another.

- The company is inside a society but that same society is inside the company. Organism and environment, company and country, are one thing. A sick country has sick companies. Sick companies—whether morally or economically ill—poison a country. The phenomenon is visible. TQM is a prescription for recovery. A form of economic penicillin, with vitamins added?

- An environment is often referred to as an *ecosystem*. The environment may be physical, chemical, geological, biological, electrical, and anything else whatsoever, in nature.

- Note that Ecology and Systems Theory are two similar if not identical disciplines. Ecology could be said to be a sub-discipline within systems theory. We mention this because systems theory and systems thinking are discussed at various points elsewhere in this manual.

- The modern study of business more and more emphasizes the intimate interconnection that must exist between an enterprise and the totality of its environment, including suppliers, competitors, customers, and supportive institutions.

- Organisms and organizations survive by drawing nourishment from the environment, in the first case food, in the second money, knowledge, and other nutrients. The organism burns up the nourishment almost as fast as it comes in. Companies, in particular, burn up money at a rapid rate—everything is an expenditure; companies do not "make" money, as Peter Drucker long ago made us realize; they simply and exclusively spend it!

- If any happens to be left over, it's gleefully referred to as a profit. Despite the glee only a very small proportion is ever left over, even in companies that are regarded as very profitable.

- It's spending that companies are good at, not profiting. In fact, the future of every company is death due to financial malnourishment; few survive for more than several decades. It's amazing how the ecological model fits both companies and creatures equally well. The question is never whether their end will come, but only "when?" In theory an eternal life is possible, but it hasn't happened yet.

- TQM is in large measure a method of designing and operating a business so that it meshes efficiently and effectively with its environment in a mutually beneficial way. It is, in other words, definitely an "ecological" approach.

- TQM recognizes the intimate symbiosis that exists between company and customer, and it knows that the customer's money is the company's vitally necessary "mother's milk." It is also a way of business that extends and prolongs corporate life.

EINSTEIN'S LAW OF LEVELS

- Albert Einstein once observed that the significant problems we face cannot be solved at the same level of thinking we were at when we created them.

- Einstein's law has considerable practical value in every field, including TQM. It enables us to take a fresh look at problems and their solutions.

- When business created its quality problem it was operating at the *level* of what has to be done by the worker *on the shop floor or in the store* to make sure that products and services go out without defects. The answer was to *set up quality **control** departments, appoint quality control supervisors, train inspectors: have a process of surveillance, monitoring and control of the workers and the production process.* But the answer created as many problems as it solved. Among these problems was the enormous cost of rejects, rework, and returns (a cost that approaches 25 percent of total wages at times), plus quality that still didn't get up to the level intended. Part of the cause was that such a regime of fear, surveillance, and policing intimidated and alienated the workers in question.

- Deming and vital others found the real solution. They discovered that it lay in changing the way that managers function. In other words, the root solution did not lie at the employee level but at the manager level. Managers had to accept a responsibility for quality. They had to change their view of employees from human objects needing control to human beings who could be creative and responsible. To accomplish this, fear and coercion had to be driven out. Managers would have to provide leadership, support, and help to the worker; they had to give the worker the quality processes and tools; and they had to provide generous training so that the worker could actually exercise initiative and become more autonomous and self-controlling.

- In short, the quality of management had to improve before the quality of the products and services could improve. Firms where the managers do not start the TQM process by looking at themselves first and altering their attitudes and behavior have no chance of going anywhere. Quality starts with the quality of management.

- Other examples of the applicability of Einstein's law can be found. For example, solving the problem at the *customer level* (through customer involvement) rather than at the *producer/deliverer* level where we originally created them. If the customer does not take part in the problem diagnosis and solution process, the solutions are unlikely to be appropriate. The customer ought to be perceived as being as much a part of the business as the managers and the employees are. Traditional managers who think they already know the customer better than the customer knows himself may have a hard time with this idea. But Einstein's law definitely suggests putting customers on our corporate boards, our strategic planning teams, and our quality action teams. After all, no customers, no business!

- Many corporate problems come from too much self-serving. TQM offers a shift toward serving others: the higher interests of the country as a whole and those of customers, suppliers, and employees—a move from the low road to the high road, to use a metaphor provided by the celebrated business author James O' Toole.

EMPOWERMENT

- Empowerment gives employees the right—within a defined framework—to make many of the decisions, and exercise many of the same initiatives as supervisors and higher levels of management.

- It implies that employees can be self-managing in the sense of setting goals, planning ahead, organizing their own work, and evaluating their own performance.

- In some instances, employee teams are permitted to be self-managing to the point of performing such managerial functions as dividing their work up as they see fit, ordering materials and supplies, and hiring new members into their team.

- Empowerment gives employees the right to deal directly, and at their own discretion, with customers and staff departments without going through their supervisors. At L. L. Bean, for example, any store clerk has the authority to replace a purchased item that a customer is dissatisfied with or make a refund without having to ask the store manager for authorization. At Delta Airlines employees make on-the-spot decisions on claims for damaged luggage, and personally put the cash in the customer's hands.

- Where substantial empowerment exists, the traditional term of "employee" often seems inappropriate and is replaced by a more descriptive nomenclature such as "associate," or some other.

- Employees have to receive substantial amounts of training, education, and coaching in order to be able to function confidently at these higher levels of authority and responsibility. The amount of training needed is a great deal more than is customary in the traditional *Just-do-as-you're-told* organizations of the pre-TQM era. Ten days per year (in perpetuity) could be considered the desired rule-of-thumb.

- Empowerment requires that a corporate climate be created in which errors are tolerated and risk-taking is both encouraged and rewarded.

- Finally, it needs to be noted that empowerment is not a matter that applies to grassroots employees only. It implies that first-level supervisors and middle managers (who are fewer in the TQM enterprise) will also act entrepreneurially, initiate changes, and spearhead innovations in their work area, and when doing so will perform as leaders, coaches, and assistants to their subordinates.

EMULATION

- The search to reach higher levels of quality and excellence in any field—from music to manufacturing, from theater to telecommunications—usually involves the searcher looking for who is best in the field, and how they do what they do.

- The purpose is not to imitate but to emulate. "Management by imitation" is by definition low-quality management. It is "monkey see, monkey do." It puts no one in the lead.

- The process of emulation can be carried out by using the TQM methodology of benchmarking.

- *Benchmarking* is a process that entails an in-depth investigation into what the excellent company is doing in order to learn from it. (See the BENCHMARKING topic for more.)

- What is learned and understood is then modified, adapted, and applied to meet the special requirements and the unique needs of the emulator.

ENERGY

- Human energy is the fuel that powers today's new vanguard style of management. This energy is multifold:
  - ➤ emotional
  - ➤ physical

- ➤ mental
- ➤ volitional (will-power)

- Jack Welch, the super-dynamic CEO of GE, says over and over again, and as emphatically as he can, that GE's survival depends on being able to release the *emotional* energy of all its people.

- The fact that the tough-minded leader of a high-technology company says he depends upon *human emotions* for the very survival of his company should be seriously reflected upon. The old mind-set that relied purely on "facts-and-logic" plus money and machines has been jettisoned by some of the most realistic executives in the land.

- This new breed of energetic, inventive, and visionary executives are not simpering Pollyannas but quite evidently people who have their heads screwed on and who have sized up the situation carefully. They claim it's not only the knowledge and intelligence that humans bring to their jobs that counts. It's what else they bring. They bring sheer animal spirit, energy, emotion, and feeling. And without these powerful human forces, the company dies!

- Note therefore that many contemporary management practices such as quality weeks, quality celebrations, quality awards, and other high-jinks have a powerful way of turning on the emotional energies of the participants. Their value is therefore inestimable.

- These cutting-edge companies also set high demands on themselves to provide facilities and training in *physical* health maintenance for employees. Employees in better health are happier, more productive and more energetic—more alive. The Roman adage of *mens sana in corpore sano*—a healthy mind in a healthy body—has been re-confirmed. Human physical energy and human emotional energy are forces that go hand in hand.

- Besides their emotional and physical energies, human beings are equipped with *mental* energies. The use of creative imagination directed toward new and better ways of doing things and

new and better things to do releases the mental energies of everyone concerned and puts it to work.

- And, finally, there is the most powerful form of human energy
  of all—*volitional* energy. Volitional energy comes from willpower
  and motivation. It is chiefly released through two mechanisms:
  empowerment and goal-setting. *Where there's a will, there's a way*—
  truer words were never said.

- Let's stop for a minute and think about this business of energy.
  Everything in the universe is driven by one or another form of
  energy. *No energy, no action.*

- Modern science and engineering methods teach us how to use
  the energy from winds, waves, sun, coal, electricity, petrochem-
  icals, and atoms. We've done such a brilliant job of producing
  and using these energies of nature that some of that power now
  threatens us. Energy is exciting stuff. But until now, we have not
  seen human energy as something that might be released with
  similar success. We realize more and more that human energy
  is also something that can be mobilized, something that can be
  employed, something that can move mountains.

ENTREPRENEURSHIP

- Under TQM, everyone is a business person—an entrepreneur—
  as well as a manager, worker, and employee of the firm.

- Entrepreneurship means finding opportunities to expand the
  business by discovering new ways and means of satisfying customers, finding new customers to satisfy.

- Training is provided on how to look for opportunities, how to
  take risks, how to overcome the fear of making mistakes, and
  how to think imaginatively.

- TQM companies often have "business incubator" systems that provide seed money for developing new business ideas. In addition,

they provide employees or managers with time away from their regular jobs to work on their entrepreneurial projects.

ETHICS

- TQM is at its heart a system of business ethics, ethics that are consciously and knowingly subscribed to.

- Its premise is that every decision is a moral and ethical decision. All decisions produce action, and all actions affect people in ways that are harmful or beneficial.

- TQM is assertively (not passively) concerned with the interests and the well-being of all the principal stakeholders—be they customers, suppliers, owners, employees, or others. It puts out energy trying to do the best it can for others, and not merely the least that is acceptable.

- TQM sees people as ends in themselves not mere means to an end, not mere "human resources." (Some TQM practitioners find the term *human resources* distasteful for this reason and will not use it as a label for human beings.)

- An increasing body of empirical research is showing that the best-performing organizations from a business point of view are ethical organizations. Unethical organizations, and amoral executives, it seems, end up doing as much damage to themselves as they do to others.

EVOLUTION OF TQM

- Although TQM has become a prominent feature of the management landscape only since about 1985, it has been practiced in whole or in part for approximately one hundred years. In its present state, it is an amalgam of many different strands woven together into one coherent pattern.

- Despite the impression given by the popular business books seen in airport newsstands, TQM is the product of no one person, or even of a small group, but represents the collective work of many brilliant contributors. The full history of management, recorded in the libraries of our universities, tells more of the whole story. Space allows reference here to only a few of the major contributors.

- TQM traces some of its roots to the early pioneers of "scientific management" such as Taylor and Gilbreth, and later to applied mathematicians such as Shewhart, Deming, and Juran—men who worked out the foundations for a science of productivity and quality improvement in the early decades of the century. (Juran, for example, was conducting quality improvement seminars as early as 1924!)

- But its eventual success depended entirely on developments that were to come later in the field of organizational behavior, psychology, and management. Deming and Juran are remarkable for the fact that their careers have spanned almost the entire history of the evolution of management!

- TQM's roots include the work of genius behavioral scientists of the 1930s such as Mayo, Roethlisberger, and Dixon of Harvard Business School, whose famed research at Western Electric revealed that the feelings and attitudes that workers held toward management were more important determinants of factory productivity than were objective matters. These attitudes were the direct result of how managers behaved toward the workers.

- Secondly, the Western Electric studies revealed that workers form themselves, unbeknownst to management, into informal small groupings under informal leaders of their own choosing, and that these groups made their own decisions about what productivity and quality were to be. In other words, long before management came up with the idea of today's "quality action teams," the apparently unorganized workers of the world already had (and still have) their own teams, whether or not management was aware of it!

- At about this same time, quite separately, Joseph Scanlon, a staff executive in the Steelworkers union, developed his system of participative management and union-management cooperation in the 1930s, based on the organization of shop-floor teams of workers and supervisors, and senior-level teams composed of workers and managers.

- The 1940s and 1950s saw the great genius Kurt Lewin do ground-breaking studies of authoritarian versus democratic leadership styles, on perception and behavior, and on resistance to change.

- Slightly later, Douglas McGregor of MIT, with his remarkable insights known as "Theory X and Theory Y," showed that the assumptions that managers make about the general character and intelligence of the employee determine how they treat employees, which in turn determines how employees respond. Theory Y managers assume that most workers are naturally responsible, energetic, ingenious, and creative unless prevented from being so by their managers. Theory X managers assume workers are not very intelligent, are motivated only by money, and respond only to rewards and punishment. They must therefore be closely supervised, monitored, and regulated.

- Most research into the relative distribution of theory X versus theory Y assumptions among managers shows that some 80 percent of North American managers favor and practice tight supervision, regulation, and control of employees, a finding that augurs poorly for any immediate large expansion of TQM and its emphasis on worker empowerment.

- From the 1930s to the 1980s Alan Mogensen, a consultant, successfully advocated a system of participative management that provided supervisors and workers with industrial engineering tools they could use to carry out "job simplification," nowadays a part of "continuous improvement" and "process engineering." Ironically, thirty and forty years later, many large corporations who had adopted Mogenson's practices, only to let them lapse despite their proved usefulness to the firm, were once again using them avidly under the umbrella of TQM, with no memory of the past.

- During the 1950s and 1960s, the idea of continuous improvement was actively promoted by leading U.S. industrial engineers and management consultants such as Professor Leo Moore of MIT. Leo Moore's cry for **"continuous improvement!"** was the slogan of the day! He promoted it at seminars all across the land. His *Harvard Business Review* articles on the matter were quoted and re-quoted. It sometimes seems true, doesn't it, that there is nothing new under the sun?

- TQM also draws on the work of the pioneers and advocates of the market-oriented and customer-centered concept of business management such as Peter Drucker and Theodore Levitt.

- It is TQM's very richness, scope, and history that lends it authenticity and strength. In the future, as in the past, it will continue to evolve and to expand in its power and flexibility.

EXCELLENCE

- *Excellence* is defined in the *Oxford English Dictionary* as *"the possession of chiefly good qualities in an eminent or unusual degree."* It defines *quality* as *"degree of excellence."*

- The quality company is one that strives for excellence in every dimension: in customer service and satisfaction, profitability, productivity, human resources, marketing, innovation, social and environmental responsibility, and so on across the entire spectrum of business functions. Quality, then, is not part of excellence—it is all of it.

EXPECTATIONS

- Expectations are a key concept in the creation and management of customer service and satisfaction. No matter how good a product or service may be in objective terms, in value for money, it will be perceived as unsatisfactory if it does not correspond with what the customer expected.

- When a customer's expectations are met, the customer is *"satisfied."* When they are not, the customer complains of being *"disappointed,"* or worse still, *"disgusted."* When they are exceeded, the customer will frequently say, *"I'm delighted!"*

- Unless they are asked, most customers will not express their satisfaction or disappointment to the provider of the product or service, but will instead express it to their friends and associates. It is said that on the average, dissatisfied customers tell two to five times as many people about their negative experiences as satisfied people tell about their positive experiences. In TQM every effort is made to find out what customers expect. A variety of methods are used, including interviews, telephone calls, focus groups, and survey questionnaires.

- Arthur Tenner and Irving DeToro, authors of the superb book, *Total Quality Management,* propose that there are four key questions that need to be asked in order to determine customer expectations:

  1. What product/service characteristics do customers want?

  2. What performance level is needed to satisfy their expectations?

  3. What is the relative importance of each characteristic?

4. How satisfied are customers with performance at the current level? (Tenner & DeToro, 1992, p. 60)

- The energetic and active investigation of what customers want, what they need, what they *could* need or want, and what they expect is a basic prerequisite to taking TQM's customer emphasis seriously. Research into customer needs and satisfactions is as fundamental a part of TQM as diagnosis is of medicine. No research, no TQM.

- TQM companies take great pains to convey to the customer information on what the customer can and cannot expect from the product or service.

- Increasingly in TQM, the strategic aim is to go beyond expectations and to create the reaction: *"I'm delighted."*

- It is not only customers who have expectations; all of the other stakeholders have theirs too. However, the thesis of TQM is that the expectations of the other stakeholders can best be met through first meeting customer expectations.

FAILURES

- Failures, or apparent failures, in TQM are many times more common than successes—ten times more.

- A common source of failure is the technocratic notion that TQM is a set of how-to-do-its that need merely be taught and put into operation by following a relatively straightforward "implementation plan." That's like having a plan to "implement" democracy, Buddhism, or racial tolerance. To adopt TQM, one must create a basic change in attitude, beliefs, and behavior. TQM initiates a powerful human and cultural change. It creates a new corporate culture and replaces an old one.

- In most, if not all cases, the failure therefore is not in TQM but in a failure to understand TQM. Things are done under the banner of TQM that betray its fundamental principles and axioms. Look before you leap.

- The quick-fix, "magic bullet" syndrome is often at work in the failure situation. The company is so much in a hurry to "implement TQM" that it doesn't take the time to research what it's all about. It is impossible to understand TQM well enough to do it by means of a two-day course, a one-week course, or even a two-week course. But people try to, and some consultants encourage them to believe they can. The truth is that it will take months of prolonged follow-up study to get to a sufficient point of understanding. One is advised, even then, to obtain experienced and qualified outside help when getting the process going.

- One trap is in the use of consultants or advisors who talk a good game, but lack the breadth and depth to be able to provide sound assistance. The motto "buyer beware" should be heeded seriously. Do a lot of reading and/or attend a few seminars before choosing your consultant. Remember that TQM truly is "total" and only advisors with a mature background of management experience can help you sort it all out. Beware those that know little beyond what's in the TQM book.

- Organizations sometimes assume that TQM will require no fundamental changes in corporate philosophy, management processes, and organizational structure and climate. When a searching re-examination is not made, and appropriate changes unrolled, there will be no environment created that can sustain the radical ideals contained in TQM.

- Classical, time-honored accounting methods, sales methods, training methods, and customary human resources are highly incompatible with TQM. Unless these functional areas are re-engineered and their methods as well as their roles transformed and altered, they will perform in ways that interfere with what is being attempted in other parts of the TQM business. The assumption that this requirement does not exist plants the seeds for many TQM failures.

FIVE RATER CRITERIA

- RATER is an acronym for "Reliability, Assurance, Tangibles, Empathy, and Responsiveness."

- It is also referred to as "servqual," an abbreviation for service quality, and as "R-rate," an acronym formed by changing the order of the five criteria: "Reliability, Responsiveness, Assurance, Tangibility, and Empathy."

- These criteria provide us with a basis for understanding what attributes make up this thing we call "service quality."

- They were developed from research done in the early 1980s by Len Berry, Parsu Parasuraman, and Valerie Zeithaml through interviews with business executives and customer focus groups. For details see their paper in the *Journal of Marketing*.

- The five criteria are actually a distillation drawn from a larger set of ten determinants of service quality that these researchers had uncovered, namely:

  - ➤ Reliability
  - ➤ Responsiveness
  - ➤ Competence
  - ➤ Access

- ➤ Courtesy
- ➤ Communication
- ➤ Credibility
- ➤ Security
- ➤ Understanding the customer
- ➤ Tangibles

FOCUS GROUP

- A small group of people—six to twelve in number—called together to give their views on a particular subject such as a product, a service, an advertisement, a plan, or anything else.

- In TQM, the focus group most often consists of a group of customers, although at times it might also be a supplier group, or a community group, or whatever, depending on the issue in question.

- In every case, the point is that the group is asked to focus their attentions and their thoughts on a particular issue and a small number (not more than five or six) of related questions.

- Focus groups have the great advantage that they bring the company and its clients (or other stakeholders) into a direct, face-to-face relationship where deeper thoughts, convictions, and feelings may be best expressed and captured.

- The information that comes from a well-conducted focus group meeting has a *qualitative* character that is enormously superior to the more *quantitative* data provided by paper questionnaires, and even telephone surveys.

- A focus group meeting typically runs about two hours, and requires the leadership of a person who is skilled in facilitation and listening.

FUTURE-FOCUSED MANAGEMENT

- TQM organizations are forward looking rather than backward looking. The minds of their people are in the future, not in the past.

- Chuck Percy, when president of Bell and Howell, had a sign on the wall behind his desk that said to all who entered his office:

  If it's not about the future of the company, I don't want to hear about it!

- The future is what is of primary concern to a person or a company. Why? Because the past cannot return. It has vanished. It is a memory. Something to treasure, to regret, to learn from. But it's not something that can be changed. As the Persian poet Omar Khayyam put it:

  The Moving Finger writes; and, having writ
  Moves on; nor all your Piety nor Wit
  Shall lure it back to cancel half a Line,
  Nor all your Tears wash out a Word of it.

- While the past is a closed book, and the present is limited, the future is wide open. It's ultimately unlimited. The future is what gives hope. The future world will be greatly different from the present, because mankind will make it so.

- But, oddly, the future is not real in the same sense that the present is real. The present is very solidly "here and now." It's "real-time," as computer people put it. At times the present may be a pleasant place to be and we enjoy it. At other times it's a pain and we endure it.

- Whether pleasant or painful, the present is always an opportunity that is continuously available—never taken away except to be instantly replaced—to do something about the future. As someone once said, the future's where we're going to spend the rest of our lives.

- Some of the future is close at hand and some of it is distant. We can look into the near future or into the far future. We can act short term or long term. Whenever we plan farther ahead than usual we can set our sights higher, because bigger things or greater things need more time and more time enables us to do bigger or greater things. A published article can be produced in a day, but a short book takes months, and a long one years. A hamburger can be put together in minutes but a gourmet meal requires a day. A small cottage can be built in a month but a big cathedral takes over a hundred years. Rome wasn't built in a day. Long-term thinkers who plan and act for the future do more and better than those who think, live, and act for the short term.

- Research studies as well as everyday evidence proves long-term thinking pays. In 1945, at the end of World War II, the just-defeated leaders of Japan set their sights on what they wanted Japan to be by the year 2000. A 55-year game plan, a preposterous idea on the surface of it, made perfect sense to them. The goal was a Japan that would by the year 2000 be number one among the world's economies. Their strategy was, as they expressed it crisply, to "build the industries of the future." Phoenix Japan would rise from the ashes of military defeat and re-create itself. The rest of the story we now know.

- With no similar game plan in hand, the world's other economies simply did not move ahead with the speed and success that Japan did. They were not future-focused. Whaling away exuberantly at the present moved the West ahead. But not at the hyper-speed of Japan.

- By the early sixties, American leaders, such as President Joseph Wilson of Xerox, were starting to get the message. By then vividly aware of what long-term thinking had done for Japan Inc., an increasing number of companies, Xerox included, decided that it would be good for their companies, too. Some, such as GE, had already committed themselves to long-term strategizing as early as the 1950s, not because of Japan but like Japan.

- Nowadays, it's axiomatic that leading-edge TQM companies need to be future-focused. A quality management team is a future-focused management team. Companies that concentrate their attention on the future are the *only* companies that will have a future.

- The future is something we should try a little less hard to predict and try a lot harder to invent. In an age of hyperchange, the erratic nature of external change makes prediction close to impossible anyway. It's now easier to create the future than forecast it. (See CREATIVITY.)

- Take an industry example of shifting attention toward the future. The desperate ten-year struggle to improve the quality of existing automobiles and to provide better quality service and superior customer satisfaction has almost been won. Classical TQM is now well established in the automobile industry. Automobile companies have begun to look farther and farther ahead, envisioning and imagining a future world of transportation that will be radically different from what now exists. A flood of new opportunities is already within view. The longer-term challenge clearly is to re-invent the automobile, to produce vehicles with bodies, power-trains, and equipment scarcely resembling those of today. The cycle that began with the early auto pioneers and innovators at the turn of this century is poised to begin all over again as we move into the next one. Perhaps we'll live to see automobiles that fly, or operate on stored-up power, or carry only one passenger, or drive themselves, or are incapable of accidents, or . . . ? They may be so different that they will no longer be called automobiles.

- How is it that humans can deal so effectively with the future when the future is something that does not yet exist? When the future is something that is expected but not present? When it is invisible to the eye, and untouchable by the hand?

- The explanation lies in the structure and design of the human brain. Over the period of two million years the human brain has evolved from an instrument not much superior to that of the ape to one that has powerful capacities. Our present generation of humans, *Homo sapiens,* is equipped with a brain with large prefrontal lobes where foresight and planning can take place.

- But our use of this cranial equipment is optional. We don't have to use it if we don't want to. The Japanese success made us aware that looking forward is not automatic but is a choice we have to make. We have an alternative choice. The alternative is to live and function only in the present and in the very short term.

- We can run our companies from financial quarter to financial quarter. We can live our lives from day to day. *Qué será, será.* In other words, we can opt not to use our frontal lobes, administering to ourselves, in effect, a non-surgical prefrontal lobotomy. What it adds up to is that we can throw away two million years of evolution.

- Or we can look ahead. Those who look ahead can draw their power from their dreams, their visions, their values, their goals, their strategies, their ideas, their images, and their plans. They can be future focused.

- There are three types of time-related managers:

  1. Those who are always behind the times in their thinking and behavior—the anachronics,

  2. Those who struggle successfully to keep up with new ideas and new realities—the synchronics, and

  3. Those who live with their minds on the future and who are ahead of the times—the metachronics.

- Another perspective on the future-focused versus present and past orientations is presented in the following diagram.

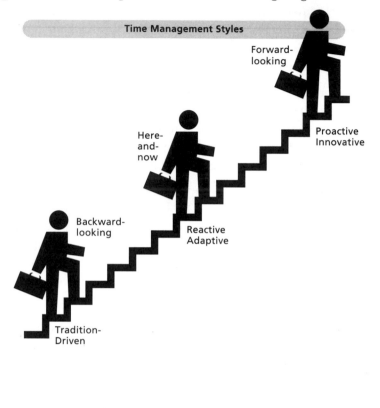

GAINSHARING

- Gainsharing is a system set up to provide financial rewards to managers and employees who form teams and networks to work together on productivity and quality-improvement programs. Some proportion of the value of the measurable gains and improvements are allocated to the managers and employees as a group, usually monthly or quarterly.

- The gainsharing system is only one component in the overall design of a broad system of worker empowerment and participation.

- Gainsharing is to be sharply distinguished from profit-sharing. Profit-sharing is seldom geared to any system of employee involvement and teamwork. It is, in most cases, a purely paternalistic and financial arrangement.

- One of the early forms of gainsharing is found in the "Scanlon Plan." This was a system of union-management cooperation invented by Joseph Scanlon while he was a member of the professional staff of the United Steelworkers, a pro-free-enterprise union. It was widely used in the U.S. steel industry during the thirties and saved many companies from bankruptcy. Other important systems include the Rucker Plan and Improshare.

- It is interesting to take the Scanlon Plan as an example of the kind of context of values and beliefs out of which the idea of gainsharing arises. The philosophical conviction behind the Scanlon Plan was that workers were eager to take on more responsibility than they had been given, were a great deal more intelligent than management had traditionally thought, and were capable of creating an unending flow of good ideas for reducing costs, streamlining work flows, and increasing quality and productivity. The basic mechanics of Scanlon's plan consisted of many small worker-manager "Productivity Committees" (today they would be called "process improvement teams"). The committees were set up in each shop in a company, along with higher-level worker-manager department committees, and a top-level company committee. The results—for cost-reduction, productivity, sales, and profits—were typically dramatic. I can't help recalling that long-ago rave story from *Fortune* on the plan called "Enterprise for Everyman"—a title that resonates extremely well with the spirit of today's TQM.

- After World War II, Scanlon was appointed a visiting lecturer at MIT and continued his work of helping companies develop systems of employee participation, involvement, and empowerment through plant floor and higher-level teams. For seven years, he was aided by Dr. George Shultz, an assistant professor of labor economics at MIT, who went on to become U.S. Secretary of Commerce and, later, Secretary of State.

- Despite the fact that case after case proved that the Scanlon system of employee empowerment and participation could help firms dramatically improve profits, productivity, wages and salaries, and enable firms to lower prices and increase market share at the same time, the percentage of North American companies that bought into the idea remained piddling. How come? Faced with the alternative of sharing power with employees or their unions, or settling for poor profits, productivity and performance, most management groups chose poor performance. Management groups can have their own management agenda, and that agenda can put their own preferences before that of any of the other stakeholders—and sometimes does. The other side of the coin has been that when faced with the choice of helping management to improve productivity and performance, or maintaining a purely adversarial relationship, some unions—not all—have preferred the adversarial posture.

- In the later forties and fifties, as part of the American policy of helping Japan in its economic recovery, the U.S. idea of a system of employee involvement and participation was explained to visiting Japanese executives who promptly took it back to Japan and put it energetically to work.

- Ironically, in the eighties and nineties the concept of employee involvement, participation, and empowerment was re-imported from Japan into the U.S. and Canada. Many mistake it for a Japanese idea. What goes around, does indeed come around!

- It took a decade of desperation to bring about a change of thinking on the part of any significant number of North American managers. The widespread media attention given to TQM firms creates an illusion that employee empowerment and involvement is in wider practice than it actually is. The reality is that most firms, hospitals, government departments, and other institutions continue to operate in an authoritarian, bureaucratic, and technocratic mode. Nonetheless TQM, involvement, and participation are spreading at a healthy rate.

GARVIN'S DIMENSIONS OF SERVICE QUALITY

- David Garvin has isolated eight dimensions for analyzing quality characteristics. The dimensions are:

  1. Performance

  2. Features: secondary aspects, "bells and whistles"

  3. Reliability

  4. Conformance to standards

  5. Durability

  6. Serviceability

  7. Aesthetics

  8. Perceived quality

- For an explanation of what each of the dimensions means the reader is referred to the explanations given on page 6 of *Total Quality Management,* by Arthur R. Tenner and Irving J. DeToro, the book mentioned earlier in the section headed EXPECTATIONS.

GOALS AND OBJECTIVES

- TQM organizations are "goal-oriented" rather than "activity-oriented." That is, they try to be as clear as possible about what they intend to accomplish.

- Goal-oriented firms use a team-based management-by-objectives process of managing in which all work activities originate in a plan of action for the achievement of an objective and the production of a result.

- Work is seen merely as a means to an end—not as an end in its own right. Work costs money. Rework costs even more!

- In TQM, no work activity is carried out for its own sake; only if it contributes to the goal by producing *a desired and intended end result.*

- In activity-oriented firms, in contrast, no conscious distinction is made between activities and goals. Many time-consuming—and therefore costly—activities are carried out without regard for their cost and their drain on the company's resources of time and talent. Activity-orientation is widespread in all institutions, including business.

- Activities become a goal in their own right. The means becomes the end. Accounting is done for the sake of accounting, training for the sake of training, advertising for the sake of advertising—all on the grounds that they are in some manner intrinsically desirable. The accounting department is judged by how well it follows proper accounting procedures. The training department is measured by how smoothly it runs courses. The advertising department is judged by whether it wins awards.

- When work is seen as a virtue in its own right, the phenomenon is known as *"the activity trap,"* to use the late George Odiorne's arresting term. Individuals are more admired for how much work they do than for what they accomplish. Since work itself is admired as much as accomplishment, no effort is ever made to eliminate it.

- In TQM, in contrast, wasteful work is the target for "search and eliminate" programs. Every effort is made to find out how to simplify—how to get things done with less work, and get them done better.

- The "effort" that TQM companies put out to eliminate and reduce work—while improving results at the same time—is purely mental. The ethic of TQM is not *"Work hard!"* but rather *"Think hard!"*

Hoshin Management

- Hoshin is a TQM-oriented system for the management of corporate change and improvement. The word *hoshin* means "a methodology for strategic direction setting."

- Invented in Japan, hoshin management (also known as hoshin kanri or policy deployment) has gone on to become popular in the United States, and has been adopted and adapted by Hewlett-Packard, Florida Power & Light, Xerox, and Intel among others. Any company venturing into TQM must become familiar with this strategically masterful methodology.

- The hoshin process begins when corporate management identifies factors that are critical to the success of the company. The identification is done through studying the environment of the business in order to recognize the specific challenges of change, and the responses that the company needs to make. Then corporate management determines exactly where improvements are needed. Improvement objectives are then formulated and "deployed" down through the company by means of specific objectives at each level that will result in the company objective being achieved. The system also tracks implementation and provides for corrective action when the objectives are not being achieved.

- For an authoritative account, see the book by Yoji Akao, *Hoshin Kanri: Policy Deployment for Successful TQM.*

- In the introduction to Akao's book, Greg Watson, now a vice president at Xerox, points out that "…hoshin kanri focuses on making competitive change—the change required to gain or maintain market position." He notes that hoshin helps to sustain competitive advantage by linking the core objectives into the current competitive situation.

- Watson also points out that the hoshin management methodology contains a built-in process through which hoshin itself is continuously reviewed. The purpose is to continuously improve the operational planning of the business rather than to leave an unquestioned, static system in place.

HUMAN QUALITIES

- The quality of the people who hold top management positions is a subject of central interest in TQM.

- Those companies headed by greed-driven, authoritarian, blaming, egocentric, tough-guy CEOs are no candidates for TQM. TQM requires the opposite: a service attitude and respect toward both customers and staff—the ethic is to give rather than to take. The ethical and responsible principles behind TQM are paramount.

- To cynics, TQM is impractically idealistic. Even advocates of TQM admit that its service ethic and its idealism pose limits on how many CEOs could honestly espouse it and perform as effective role models.

- The human qualities most conducive to top management TQM leadership are conscience, integrity, vision, and respect for people.

- Human quality is important in all fields, not only business and government. For example, in team sports, Wayne Gretsky serves as a role model of the "quality athlete" because of the way in which he combines high performance and a good nature.

HUMOR

- Some TQM companies consider humor to be important.

- Having a good laugh is one of the best ways there is to release tension and reduce the stress of today's highly kinetic, sometimes frenetic, business world.

- High-performance teams often find that they have the good fortune to contain at least one member who has the happy aptitude for relieving tension from time to time with a humorous remark or wisecrack.

- The philosopher-writer Arthur Koestler has also demonstrated that creative thinking and humor share in common the fact that they employ offbeat thinking. Both creative thinking and humor employ unexpected, off-tangent connections among facts and ideas. Whether "ah-ha!" or "ha-ha!" the result of both is discovery or insight.

- Any time a team is percolating with new ideas, the sound of laughter never stops; it just can't be helped.

- It's no surprise that creative business people almost always have a streak of humor. The overly serious are rarely inventive at anything, however admirable, reliable, or sound they likely are.

- On top of it all, the ability to laugh at oneself is generally regarded by psychologists as essential to mental health and the preservation of sanity.

- It's been suggested that today's companies could do worse than hire a "court jester" to keep the level of stress down and the level of creativity up.

- It's a bit odd to talk this seriously about humor, but there you are.

HYPERCHANGE

- Hyperchange is the new change that surrounds us today.

- It combines the three classical types of change—linear, exponential, and discontinuous—with a new type, *chaotic change,* which is random and unpredictable.

- A major characteristic of hyperchange is the rate at which things—states, nations, corporations, products, product models, books, magazines, fashions, ideas—abruptly disappear and are replaced by other things.

- The hardest truth that hyperchange confronts us with is *nothing is forever.* Everything is temporary. Things appear. Things disappear. The hyperchange process of chronic *appearances and disappearances* creates a new world order different from anything that ever existed. A world of the provisional and the transient.

- The emotional and spiritual challenges of hyperchange are enormous. Confusion and uncertainty abound. Many things appear more ambiguous and more complex. Fear and anxiety are chronic responses. Hyperchange therefore calls for a new mind-set, for a re-examination of fundamental values, for new attitudes, and new ways of functioning.

- Unlike linear and exponential change, the random and erratic components of hyperchange mean that much that is important cannot be predicted, planned or controlled. So more rapid, flexible, and intuitive responses are often needed to deal with an ever-surprising new reality. Response speed becomes a survival ability, agility an imperative. A rereading of Alvin Toffler's *Future Shock* is advisable.

IDEA-DRIVEN MANAGEMENT

- TQM is part of a new management paradigm that makes conscious use of human intelligence. TQM firms are deliberate users of thought and thinking, of concepts and ideas. Ideas cover a large spectrum and appear in such various forms as conjectures, thoughts, convictions, possibilities, methods, strategies, solutions, and plans.

- A TQM firm is always driven by two or three big ideas that give it focus and meaning and form the basis for its success.

- General Electric is driven by the idea that if you can't be number one or two in a field you shouldn't be in it because you lack the ability to compete without killing yourself; get out of that field and get into some field you are really good at.

- Apple Computer is driven by the idea that if you want to sell a lot of computers you'd better make them user friendly.

- McDonald's is driven by the idea, among others, that if your restaurant isn't squeaky clean you'll lose customers by the droves.

- Carrier Corporation is driven by the idea that to succeed and survive it has to put the interests of the customer first and make the goal of profit subordinate. The same idea, clearly announced, dominated AT&T for generations.

- Texas Instrument's history has been dominated by the idea that every employee should be a manager, be trained in management, and manage their own work. (That idea was made a reality dozens of years ago, long before the present-day empowerment movement took form.)

- How about the traditional firm? Traditional firms, run by old-style traditional managers, operate by habit, custom, procedure, and convention, with little regard for ideas. Conceptual thinking just isn't part of it. Independent thinking does not play any part when things are being done. They're done by rote, mechanically, and mindlessly. If asked why a thing is done, the answer is *"Just do it. It's policy,"* or, *"Because we've always done it that way."*

- Idea-driven TQM companies are forever looking for new ideas about what to do and about how to do it. They urge everyone to "think" and to "work smart." They provide training in analytical and creative thinking, and in decision-making. They teach how to practice foresight and exercise imagination. They provide training in how to sell ideas, get support for ideas, and put ideas successfully to work.

- Idea-driven firms are people-oriented. They are convinced that the most important factor in business is people—the minds and hearts of people. They value human character, will, and courage. They value intelligence.

- TQM's success depends—absolutely and totally—on the ability of the people in the enterprise, from CEO to truck-driver, to generate new and different ideas for better things to do and better ways to do them. Idea-driven companies *believe* in ideas, *use* them, and *produce* them. They ask for ideas. They pay for them. They reward them. They make money from them.

- Ideas have the power to move the world. H. G. Wells, the great British historian, claimed that *"the history of the world is a history of ideas"*—the idea of democracy, the idea of voting, the idea of universal education, the idea of saving, the idea of agriculture, the idea of the plow, the idea of the wheel, the idea of a personal computer.

- Concepts and ideas may vary from very large ones like democracy, freedom, delegation, participation, leadership, entrepreneurship, corporate culture (to pick out a few) to important but more mundane ones like portability, fast delivery, safety-first, or what have you.

- Total Quality Management itself has been one of the biggest and most influential of all the great ideas in the entire history of management. Most of us would agree with the proposition that TQM is *an idea whose time has come.*

- TQM is a very close neighbor to another historically great idea, that of excellence—an idea and an ideal that has made some individuals, some institutions, and some nations great.

- Ideas are so powerful that we need to pay more attention to what they are and where they come from.

- Their source and location is the human brain. They are produced in the cerebral cortex by the process we know as "thought" or "thinking," and can be held there for consideration and possible employment.

- A new idea is generated by challenging any and all established practices. It is not respectful of the status quo. It questions things. A direct and simple procedure for challenging the status quo is to ask the simple question "why?" and then ask it several times again. Some Japanese firms suggest asking "why" five times in a row, challenging each successive answer as it comes forward.

- The habit-driven style, which TQM replaces, consisted of finding something worth doing, finding a way to do it, and then using this same way forever. It then becomes the traditional, established, accepted way. It becomes the "right" way, the "correct" way, the unquestioned way. Carrying it out can be automatic, and require little if any thought. It is a hazard to survival.

- We humans realize our full potential when we use our intelligence to become more conscious and aware of what is being done around us and what we ourselves are doing.

IDEAL SOLUTION

- A method sometimes used to achieve a higher level of quality and excellence is to visualize what would be the ideal and perfect product, service, company, or whatever.

- For example, MBA student Fred Smith, had a vision of the perfect or idealized rapid, overnight parcel delivery system for the U.S. It consisted of a system in which parcel-carrying planes would fly to a central hub from places all over the country. The parcels would be unloaded then reloaded onto outbound planes flying out to all the different destinations. This idealized, perfect system became a reality when Federal Express came into existence.

- Success is often the result of visualizing the ideal and the perfect, and then trying to attain it. For example, McDonald's restaurants achieve a speed of service, a quality of service, a degree of cleanliness, and a level of pricing that is hard to fault.

- Sometimes imagining ("imaging"?) the ideal—and pursuing it—leads to achieving a level of accomplishment and quality that had previously seemed unrealistic.

- The technique is less than new, having been invented by Plato in Athens four hundred years before Christ. The technique has proved its use again and again over many centuries, and can therefore be said to be well tested. Try it. It has amazing power.

IMAGINATION

- No one questions in this age of information, communication, and knowledge whether the facts, information, and knowledge being made available are valuable and important. But what is being questioned is whether information, facts, and knowledge are enough. The conclusion being reached more and more through research and observation is that they are not, and that our real successes come through the exercise of imagination.

- Imagination plays a huge role in every aspect of today's new vanguard management style, ranging from how to imaginatively create new images of quality to how to imaginatively invent new products and services.

- Indeed, the value being placed on imagination in business stands side by side with the value that has always been placed on imagination in the world of the arts.

- Many of the facts and the realities that the hard-nosed, analytical, and empirical school of thinking pay great respect to are now recognized to be the result of images first produced by the human imagination. For example, the world produces billions of light bulbs annually and lights the world with them. But we need to remember that the idea of the light bulb preceded the light bulb and not vice-versa. The fertile imagination of Edison conceived of both the bulb and the General Electric company that makes them! The idea of the United Nations preceded the existence of the United Nations.

- In terms of what comes first, imagination or facts, we now realize that we have had the cart before the horse! The fact is, imagination precedes fact. This is what Einstein meant when he said, *"In science, imagination is more important than knowledge,"* and what Napoleon meant when he claimed that *"Imagination rules the world"*!

- The role of imagination in ordinary life is even more basic than its association with art, invention, and innovation suggests. Before we do such a simple act as going out to lunch, the image of going out flashes through our imaginations, however fleetingly or dimly. In more important things, imagination is a lot more active—it's hard for it not to be. The young person who decides to become an engineer or a doctor imagines himself or herself in the role. The reality when they experience it will, of course, be a lot different from what they had imagined! Just the same, without the image no action would ever take place. All of which adds up to saying that imagination is no idle add-on to the human mind but a basic part of what a person needs to function at all.

- Nothing will convince the "down-to-earth" type of person better about the importance of imagination than what has been discovered about how successful achievers use it. David McLelland and a large research team at Harvard, funded with several million dollars of research money, did exhaustive work on the subject of achievement. The research stretched over a twenty-year period. The researchers found that in every field, from sports to business to science or whatever, achievers are not merely doers but dreamers. In contrast, non-achievers, no matter how busy, diligent and hardworking, are not dreamers. The researchers found that high achievers in every field engage in "chronic fantasizing." Achievers were always looking ahead, imagining what they could accomplish, and visualizing (strategizing) how to accomplish it. Achievers were also action-oriented—they did what had to be done to make the dream come true. McLelland and his team discovered that they could teach non-achievers how to become achievers. The method was to teach non-achievers how to visualize a goal, and then how to visualize getting to that goal.

- Imagination is not an Aladdin's lamp that produces results without effort. Edison tested thousands of filaments before finding one that worked. Small wonder he said that *"Genius is one per-cent inspiration and ninety-nine percent perspiration."* Imagination may give us the design for the house but it doesn't build it. (Sorry to come back down to earth this way!)

IMPROVEMENT METHODOLOGIES

- The phrase *improvement methodologies* refers to the family of meth-ods that are used in continuous quality improvement. They include the following commonly used methods among others:

  - ➤ Hoshin management
  - ➤ Quality function deployment
  - ➤ Benchmarking
  - ➤ Cost of quality
  - ➤ New management and planning tools
  - ➤ Customer surveys
  - ➤ Value-added management
  - ➤ Customer-producer-supplier linking
  - ➤ Business re-engineering
  - ➤ Cycle time reduction
  - ➤ Statistical methods
  - ➤ Work flow analysis
  - ➤ Just-in-time
  - ➤ QC tools
  - ➤ Process improvement methods
  - ➤ Design for manufacturing and assembly
  - ➤ Continuous flow manufacturing
  - ➤ Mistake-proofing devices

INFORMATION

- TQM organizations analyze their information flows with the same diligence as their process flows.

- Information is the transformation of data into useful forms. Information is what gives form, pattern, and meaning to data.

- Information, knowledge, and knowledge workers constitute over 90 percent of the resources of many large organizations.

- In almost all of today's firms, information and knowledge are of prime strategic importance. Achieving a high level of excellence in a firm's information management capabilities is one of the prime objectives of TQM.

- The purpose is to ensure that the right value-adding information is available to the right people at the right time.

- The value that is added at each step in a company's value-adding chain is largely created by the application of information, ideas and knowledge.

- Knowledge and information are increasingly the principal sources of corporate strength and economic power. A key strategic resource in modern business.

- Defects and disorders in the technical and moral quality of information come into existence as a result of misinformation, disinformation, information overload, information pollution, industrial espionage, patent infringements, copyright violations, plagiarism, and fraud.

INITIATIVE

- Under TQM, everyone in the rank-and-file is encouraged and enabled to think and act for themselves—to be proactive rather than reactive. They do not need to wait for instructions, requests, or recommendations to come from others when circumstances require action to be taken. They simply do it. They act.

- They regard themselves not as objects to be acted upon, but as causal agents who can act autonomously. They can get things done that need to be done. They can produce the new ideas that need to be produced.

ISO

- ISO stands for "International Standardization Organization."

- It provides a series of quality standards referred to as ISO 9000, accepted by 92 countries.

- ISO 9001 covers **product** design and development; ISO 9002 is for production and installation operations.

- To meet the needs of today's more service-based economy, a new program, ISO 9004-2, was created to provide **service** organizations with the special kind of quality criteria they particularly need.

- A paperback ($235. 00—yes, you read right), the *ISO 9000 Compendium,* details the standards and can be obtained from American National Standards Institute in New York City; telephone 212-642-4900).

- Companies that can demonstrate that they follow required procedures for meeting ISO standards can apply for and receive an ISO certificate, which will register them as ISO companies. Some purchasers will do business only with ISO registered suppliers. As of 1993, about 30,000 companies worldwide had been certified.

JURAN TRILOGY

- The Juran trilogy, formulated by Dr. Joseph M. Juran, one of the great pioneers of quality management, asserts that there are three "management processes" essential to quality achievement:

  ➤ Quality planning
  ➤ Quality control
  ➤ Quality improvement.

- As part of the improvement process, Juran advocates the identification of team "projects." The idea is that needed improvements can be singled out—those which are in line with corporate strategy—and teams can then be organized to work on these strategically important improvement projects.

KNOWLEDGE WORKERS

- Knowledge worker describes a person who works with information, ideas, and knowledge. Examples are engineers, systems analysts, personnel specialists, graphic artists, writers, publishers, and TQM handbook editors.

- To an increasing extent, the quality of an organization's products and services is a function of the quality of its knowledge workers and the quality of the work they do.

- Knowledge workers are paid for what they know as well as for what they do. They are characterized by having an advanced level of training and education.

- Knowledge workers constitute an increasing percentage of the post-industrial workforce.

- Their tools and equipment are the telephone, the fax, the computer, the video, and the communication-computer network. These comprise the hard technologies of their trade.

- The soft technologies they use consist of the procedures, techniques, and methodologies of their particular occupations, e.g., in human resources management, accounting, marketing, engineering, and so on.

- Due to the ever-advancing growth of knowledge, knowledge workers exist in constant danger of falling behind, and are in constant need of skill and knowledge upgrading. Obsolescence threatens them in the same way that arthritis threatens the logger or loss of appetite the sumo wrestler. Every occupation has its hazards.

- One of the greatest forces for change in the direction of egalitarianism is the emergence of the knowledge economy. In knowledge-based firms, the managers simply have to accept the worker's judgments on many things.

- In some firms, management succeeds in making the firm successful only to the degree that it can manage to attract and hold the best knowledge workers. No matter how you put it, this means that while admitting that the workers have to please the managers , the managers also have to please the workers—certainly those they wish to retain.

- Employment in professional firms—engineering firms, law firms, management consultancies, etc. —represents the far end of this scale. Typically, the "employees" own the firm, manage it, and do its work.

- Some large professional firms have decided to manage themselves in a TQM manner. While conducting a TQM seminar for the senior consultants in a management consulting firm in England recently, the president told me that the entire international organization of this U.S.-based multinational was in the process of moving in the TQM direction.

- Large professional firms, with as many as five or ten thousand or more members, are a reflection of the new society and the new economy and the reliance on information, knowledge, and brainpower. The rise of the large professional firm is considered such a significant phenomenon that the University of Western Ontario offers a second-year MBA course on the subject, taught by Dr. John Howard, who is the leading global researcher, writer, and consultant in this exciting new field of management study.

LEADERSHIP

The real test of quality in the early part of the next century is going to be . . . the quality of leadership.
BOB GALVIN (FORMER CEO OF MOTOROLA)

The wicked leader is he who the people despise. The good leader is he who the people revere. The great leader is he of whom the people say, "We did it ourselves."
LAO TSU

- In TQM, everybody, employee and manager alike, is expected to exercise leadership whenever the situation is appropriate.

- Since TQM relies heavily on Improvement Teams, Project Teams, and Innovation Teams, team leadership skills must become part of everyone's training.

- Every employee is also a manager with a particular zone of responsibility to manage.

- In addition, every employee is encouraged to be entrepreneurial—that is, to be creative, enterprising, and innovative.

- Every person in the company has a three-dimensional role as leader, manager, and entrepreneur-innovator.

- The TQM company provides training in how to function effectively in all three of these roles.

- Vision, dedication, courage, compassion, fortitude, and imagination are the required character traits of every employee-manager-innovator. They transcend the requirements traditionally expected from those who used to function only in the classical plan-and-control mode.

LEARNING

- Learning includes the acquisition of new information, knowledge, skills, strategies, abilities, attitudes, habits, insights, realizations, convictions, values, and beliefs.

- Learning has a new strategic importance in today's business world. Corporate education and training have attained a position of prominence in today's management priorities.

- In the hyperchange world of today, the ability or willingness to learn new things becomes as critical as the ability or skill to do things after they have been learned. Earning a living becomes a matter of "learning a living."

- Knowledge and skills become rapidly obsolete. As far back as 1960, the Bell Telephone Company of Canada estimated that the half-life of an engineering degree was five years. The half-life means the amount of time it takes for 50 percent of something to disappear.

- New knowledge is being generated at a phenomenal rate in every field and discipline. In some exceptionally knowledge-intensive industries, learning consumes *half or more of the available time of the staff.*

- However, subject matter is not the whole of it. Learning may occur at many different levels: simple or complex, easy or difficult, fast or slow, and superficial or deep.

- Learning can be emotional and behavioral as well as mental and intellectual. It can result, at its ultimate, in personal transformations, altered understandings, and wholly new views of reality. Learning at these levels has to be very much a self-motivated matter.

- Organizations that want to go TQM have to invest heavily in educational and training programs, some of a technical and practical nature and others of an attitudinal, social, and behavioral nature. The training covers everything from statistics to creativity and risk-taking, and the investment can go as high as four or five percent of payroll over a sustained period of three years.

- The resulting improvements in performance, productivity, self-fulfillment, effectiveness, and profits have been proven to pay the investment back many times over.

LEARNING ORGANIZATIONS

- Think of organizations as giant organisms learning from their environment and acting on their environment—sometimes successfully and sometimes not. They learn their environment, they learn *from* their environment. In a way, they are like scientists conducting a laboratory experiment.

- On the basis of their actions and the resultant feedback, organizations acquire new insights into the environment and how it behaves. They then adapt and modify their behavior, acquire new skills, build new perceptions and understandings, and continue this process of growth and learning in perpetuity, changing and altering as the environment changes and alters.

- The cardinal point to remember in the theory of the learning organization, is that corporate learning is not merely a classroom process. It is much more than the acquisition of information, knowledge, and know-how, although it does encompass such formal types of learning. The concept of the learning organization deals with something deeper.

- The concept of the learning organization arises from the idea that not only individuals but also small groups and large organizations can learn, and organizational learning is much more than the sum total of individual learning.

- The central idea is that learning organizations learn how to change their thinking, their strategies, their structures, and their processes in order to stay up with or get ahead of changes in their environments, and learn better ways of interacting and living within their environments.

- Learning organizations not only acquire knowledge, information, and know-how but they create and invent it themselves; although doing so for their own benefit, they inevitably contribute to the knowledge and wisdom of the whole society.

- The innovative organization is the ultimate or most advanced stage in the evolution of learning organizations; in a sense their very business is learning, learning how to create new things and new services in new ways.

- The idea of the "learning organization" appeared in print as early as 1970 in *The Future Society,* a book edited by American social scientist and cyberneticist Donald N. Michael.

- An excellent depiction of the comprehensive way in which learning organizations learn can be found in the short and very readable book called *The Learning Company,* by Mike Pedler, John Burgoyne, and Tom Boydell. As these authors put it:

  A learning company is an organization that facilitates the learning of all its members and continuously transforms itself. . . . This is the dream—that we can design and create organizations which are capable of adapting, changing, developing, and transforming themselves in response to the needs, wishes, and aspirations of people, inside and out. (Pedler, Burgoyne, and Boydell, 1991, p. 1)

- A fundamental postulate in the concept of the learning organization is that through mistakes we learn, both as individuals and as organizations. When mistakes are made and recognized, something new can then be tried. Trial-and-error experimentation is a necessary part of learning.

- Advocates of the error-embracing philosophy of the learning organization have jokingly suggested that the following warning be posted on corporate bulletin boards:

NO MORE MISTAKES, AND YOU'RE OUT!

- While it is obviously undesirable to make mistakes whenever we are producing or delivering the final good or service to the customer, it's rarely possible to avoid them when we're engaged in a learning, discovery, or development process.

- James Bere, chairman of Borg-Warner, puts it this way:

  Most people do not want to take the risk of failure, and therefore they do not want their people to make mistakes. And I say it's the absolute reverse. You do not develop a quality person without making mistakes. (Potts & Behr, 1987, p. 77)

- Healthy organizations can and do learn just as individuals can and do. Unhealthy organizations with fixed ideas and stale notions, closed minds, obsolete skills, and old habits, do not learn, do not adapt, and do not survive. The evidence of this truth is everywhere around us.

- The learning organization thrives through curiosity, open-mindedness, a disposition to reflect upon experience, a willingness to challenge old ideas, and a readiness to entertain new ones.

- A company whose corporate and departmental walls are impermeable—closed off from the universal explosion of new ideas and new knowledge—becomes uncompetitive and obsolete.

- As yesterday's strategies and policies become irrelevant, new ones need to be found. Obsolete practices need to be junked in the same way as obsolete machinery.

- The learning organization adapts superbly to change. It examines itself for deficiencies. It seeks and acquires new solutions. It modifies its strategies to suit changing prospects and realities.

- In all these various ways, the TQM organization can be said not only to learn, but to learn through being intelligent and aware

- TQM companies maintain and advance their level and scope of quality and excellence by corporate learning that is both energetic and ceaseless. To such companies, TQM is not a mere set of established methods and procedures to be implemented but a profound commitment to discovery, exploration, learning, experimentation, entrepreneurship, and innovation.

LINKAGES

- Linkages refer to the connections that take place between suppliers, manufacturers, distributors, retailers, and servicing that arise in the value-adding chain, in the sequence of activities that begins with raw materials and ends with a product or service received by a consumer and in use.

- It also refers to the linkages that take place within the firm between design, engineering, purchasing, manufacturing, marketing, and distribution.

- Although these linkages should be well-integrated backwards and forwards, in practice they often are disjointed and counterproductive—i.e., the left hand does not know what the right hand is doing.

- Examples are products designed in such a way that they are difficult to handle and service, branch banks that lose customers because loans are too slowly processed at headquarters, plants that are understaffed because the human resources department is not training replacement workers fast enough, and so on.

- TQM is a "systems" approach to business that concentrates on bringing about integration, teamwork, and consistency among these groups and their interdependent activities.

- The result is often enormous gains in effectiveness, efficiency, speed, quality, and improvements in end-user satisfaction.

LISTENING

- Traditional management practices have always emphasized *telling*. TQM emphasizes *listening*.

- Instead of having managers who tell their subordinates what to do and how to do it, TQM managers ask their subordinates what *they* think and what *they* want to do.

- Instead of having salespersons who try to talk at the customer and try to push or persuade the customer to buy, TQM companies listen to the customer and provide the customer only with what the customer *wants* to buy.

- TQM companies provide training in how to listen, a training made necessary because most people have been taught all their lives to do the opposite, indeed often to believe that to listen to other's viewpoints is a sign of weakness rather than strength.

- The rules for listening are:

  ➤ Ask the other person what they think and feel.

  ➤ Listen with attention to what they say, paying attention also to what they do not say.

  ➤ Listen to the feelings they are expressing as well as to the information or opinions they are conveying. Do not argue; do not interrupt.

  ➤ From time to time, see if you are reading them right by repeating back to them the gist of what you think they have been communicating. (Often you will have misunderstood!)

MANAGEMENT PROCESS

- TQM organizations have a *conscious and deliberate* process for the managing of the business in a results-oriented manner. All of the managers of all divisions, departments, and units use this process.

- Whatever specific form it takes in a given company, this management process consists of:

  ➤ defining the business and its clients

  ➤ formulating a mission and role

  ➤ identifying goals and objectives

> developing strategies and plans for achieving them

> assembling the necessary resources

> organizing and coordinating people and processes

> implementing the plan of action

> observing, monitoring, and measuring results

> taking corrective actions to modify the objectives, the resources, the organization, the plan, or the implementation

MBOR

- MBOR means *management by objectives and results*. It is sometimes referred to simply as "management by objectives" and sometimes as "management by results," depending on which side of the MBOR coin is facing you.

- An objective is the mental image—the picture you have in mind—of some intended result. For example, the image of owning a new house, of having a bigger bank account, of achieving an increase in sales, of having an improved product for customers, of having a better factory to work in, etc. If you want to produce a result, you start with a picture—for example, you want to have a circle on a piece of paper, you see a circle in your mind before you draw it. MBOR is a visualization process.

- A leading management thinker and consultant of the fifties, E. C. Schleh, was among the earliest of modern proponents of the idea that managers ought to concentrate their attention first on what *results* they intended to produce, and only then on *how* to produce them. Means—the how-to's—should be subordinated to ends. Schleh believed many companies do the opposite. They were very busy doing a multitude of things with great proficiency, yet unclear just exactly what results they were after. Much action but not much results. And all due to not starting out with a clear picture in mind of what the objectives were, what results they aimed to produce. With Schleh's notion in mind, try this. Ask the next person you meet to describe three objectives they're pursuing. They'll probably tell you what they're *doing*, rather than what *results* they're pursuing. Then ask yourself the same question. The goal-oriented, MBOR way of functioning doesn't come instinctively, it seems; we have to be conscious that that's the way we want to operate.

- Peter Drucker's research in the early fifties on the phenomenon of corporate success lead him to the discovery that high performing firms like Du Pont and GM based their management style on the principle of having clearly formulated objectives. What successful corporations accomplished, Drucker found, was what they expressly *intended* to accomplish. The intention was the driving force. It means being proactive as against reactive. They had goals and objectives.

- MBOR is more than a procedure; it is a philosophy, an attitude, and a management practice. The empowering idea—the fundamental concept—behind the management-by-objectives methodology has been known throughout history as *intentionality*. The thought is that while some things just happen, other things can be made to happen, consciously, deliberately, willfully, and intentionally.

- When you do things intentionally, then, you do them in order to produce some desired result or effect. We're talking about good, old-fashioned willpower. Willing things to be what we want them to be. We're talking about the quite amazing power of the human will.

- The principle of setting goals and objectives as a means of bringing about intended success is not new. It was first formulated by Aristotle, several hundred years before the birth of Christ. Later, it was subsequently espoused by a succession of political, military, and commercial leaders over the centuries, continuing down to this day.

- Military strategists, for example, have long based their strategies and planning on what they term *the principle of the objective*—long before the use of objectives became popular in the business world. (For that matter, "strategy" was a concept and a way of thinking that has been used in the military for centuries. But it has been in use in the business world for less than thirty years now. Hard to believe, but true. Dictionaries of thirty years ago describe strategy exclusively as a military idea.)

- Today, in contemporary MBOR, the company has objectives, the division has objectives, the department has objectives, the unit has objectives, and the team has objectives. In addition, individuals have objectives. In some more limited forms of MBOR, concern is only or mainly with the individual and his/her objectives, but TQM requires the more inclusive contemporary approach.

- In the TQM approach to MBOR, the following principles govern:

    1. Missions, visions, roles, goals and objectives will be the beginning points for all planning. They are the expression of *purposefulness*. Whatever we do, there should be a purpose to it.

    2. *Objectives, in this light, are a means to the higher purposes of survival, success, service, and growth and development.* They are not the final end to which we are moving.

    3. Objectives can be formulated only after the overall organization's mission, vision and strategies have been articulated by the Board and the top management team.

    4. A team approach is also followed when first the company and then the divisions, departments, and units explore specific challenges and opportunities, set their objectives, and develop their plans.

    5. Objectives are set with respect to customer service and satisfaction, quality, productivity, time intervals, cycle time, technology, innovation, profitability, and all stakeholder interests.

6. Objectives will be specific, challenging, attainable, and their achievement should be verifiable either through measurement or through first-hand observation and judgment.

7. An objective, to repeat, will be regarded as a *future-intended result,* that is, a result to be produced by some given date in the future, whether that date is a few days, or a few years off, or much farther off. This *forward-looking mind-set* and future-focused approach is one of the intrinsic features of today's management style.

8. The purpose of having objectives is to be able to produce worthwhile results. The results are what count.

9. But there is one thing that must be remembered. Human action always—repeat, *always*—produces unintended as well as intended results. This is known as the *principle of unintended consequences.* Half the principle is contained in the old dictum that said *"The path to hell is paved with good intentions."* The City Fathers of Atlanta decided many years ago to build a highway intended to accommodate traffic twenty years into the future. Within four years it was overcrowded. The highway had the unintended consequence of causing a boom in suburban development. On the other hand, unintended consequences can be desirable. Some time ago, a company took out an option on a large tract of land where it thought it might locate a production site. Instead they made themselves a fortune when land prices exploded—right after the government had decided, to the company's happy surprise, to run a highway through the center of the tract.

10. Objectives can be short term, medium term, or long term.

11. Objectives will be flexible. When circumstances change, objectives can be altered. Activities and processes that do not contribute to corporate objectives, responsibilities, and results are deleted in order to eliminate waste, and free up resources for productive re-deployment.

- A mere "written objective"—a statement on a piece of paper—has no meaning whatsoever unless it corresponds to an actual image or idea firmly held in someone's mind. Unfortunately paper statements are often taken to be the equivalent of true objectives, a delusory state of affairs that would be similar to mistaking the picture of an automobile for the automobile itself.

- Any company where MBO or MBOR has become an elaborate procedure entailing lengthy documents and/or a control orientation, or where its prime purpose is performance appraisal, has a false—perverted—form of MBO/MBOR, one that would be fundamentally counterproductive to TQM. MBO/MBOR was intended to replace bureaucracy by simplicity and external control by self-control, not to create more of both.

MCL GRID

- The MCL Quality Grid, shown below, is an experimental tool that we have developed at our company, Management Concepts Limited, for training and research purposes. Its aim is to provide *a different kind of paradigm* for looking at quality, a paradigm that places greater emphasis than customary on the subjective aspect of how customers experience the product or service, and how they feel and think about it.

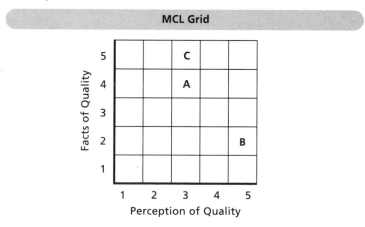

- What this paradigm implies, among other things, is that the same product or service is perceived as having a much *different* quality depending on who's buying or using it.

- It also implies that as TQM evolves it should or will be focusing more concern on the great need for getting inside the customer's skin and seeing and feeling things through the customer's eyes and heart.

- The hope is that the MCL grid will help designers and deliverers of products and services get a deeper insight into the elusive interplay between the *objective* (factual/visible) aspects that everyone can agree upon (more or less) and the *subjective* effects that are produced within the customer and are not visible.

- The MCL grid can be used as an investigative tool by companies who want to determine what the customers' quality expectations are, and how they measure their satisfactions and dissatisfactions. The research could be done with individual customers or, perhaps better still, with focus groups where subjective processes of evaluation can be better brought out into the open.

- The following shoot-from-the-hip examples illustrate how the instrument can be employed.

  ➤ *CASE A:* The customer in question has accounts at several different banks. He is less than delighted with the quality of service at one of them, despite rating it a four on all factual factors such as accuracy, range of products, speed, etc. He rates it three at best on certain subjective factors. He has had an account at the branch for fifteen years, solely because of its convenient location. Normally, most of the staff are new and don't recognize his face, never mind know him by name. The staff are always very busy-looking, seem pressed for time, and show little if any personal interest in the customers. They have little interest in their personal appearance and are poorly groomed. The tacky wall ads and untidy decor also irk him.

  ➤ *CASE B:* After much difficult searching a couple was very pleased to find the two-piece couch that fit exactly into the corner of the small den where they watched television in the evenings. It was soft, comfortable, roomy, and decorated in a fabric they liked. In terms of the subjective or perceived quality they rated it an unquestionable five. But the couch cushions soon lost their elasticity and the fabric wore out sooner than normal. Furthermore, when they took the couch to be reupholstered the underlying materials were sub-standard and the workmanship lacking. They rated it two on the factual and objective aspects of quality.

➤ *CASE C:* The family subscribes to two newspapers. The first is a national newspaper, which they rate five on the factual scale for its scope, depth, detail, and rigor. They rate it only three on several subjective and perceived dimensions. They describe the paper as superior and condescending, coolly detached from social problems, self-absorbed and self-congratulatory, and snobbishly elitist. Instead of being delivered right to their front door the paper is tossed onto the driveway, near the garage, a good fifty feet away. They rate the other, a city newspaper, only two on the objective and factual scale of qualities but five on its humanity and its concern for the customer. The paper is brought right to the house and placed with care inside the storm door. If placed on the grid, it would occupy a different square.

• When actually employing the grid for serious business purposes, a more refined approach would be to begin with a careful listing of the objective (factual) variables and the subjective (perceived) quality variables that enter into the assessment we make of the quality of the object, service or person concerned. Then rate the quality of each of the objective and subjective variables on a one to five scale, calculate the average, and position the result in the grid.

• The grid is a new tool that is yet to go through several stages of improvement and development. In the usual TQM spirit of supplier-client partnering, we would welcome ideas, contributions, and examples of how it is being used by you.

- For readers who want to look more deeply into the human and subjective aspects of quality and customer satisfaction, we heartily recommend Karl Albrecht's book, *The Only Thing that Matters— Bringing the Power of the Customer into the Center of Your Business.* Albrecht emphasizes more than any other writer the fact that it is how the customer is made to feel that counts, that feelings are the governing factor. It's a book that gets you truly inside the customer's heart and mind.

Measurement

- Measurement is an essential ingredient in the TQM process, at every stage.
- The following concept of "levels of measurement" can therefore be looked at as a necessary tool for anyone wanting to manage in the TQM manner. It is adapted from Tenner and DeToro, 1992, p. 44.

Three Levels of Quality Management

Process Measures
Activities, variables and operations of the process itself

Output Measures
Specific features, values, attributes and characteristics of the product or service

Outcome/Results Measures
Effects on customers and customer satisfaction

SOURCE: Reprinted with permission of Irving DeToro, The Quality Network, Ltd.

MIND-SET

- The desire to achieve a globally competitive level of quality is not sufficient for actually achieving it. It depends on a mind-set different from the one most managers have had in the past.

- The term "management mind-set" refers to the way in which a manager sees the world as a whole and how it works, including business and management itself.

- Part of the TQM mind-set is that globally high standards can be reached only when management believes that employees are as capable of achievement as are managers.

- Putting the customer first is another element in the mind-set necessary for TQM, and the achievement of global levels of competitiveness.

- The charismatic president of one TQM company, United Technologies Carrier, has had a page-size mirror included into one of the booklets the company provides to its managers. It's his way of suggesting that managers take a look at themselves, become more self-aware.

- A change in mind-set—because it is something that lies deep within a person—can be difficult, and sometimes painful.

- However, the success of companies such as Ford and Xerox and others shows that a change in management mind-set is possible providing the will to change exists.

- Since TQM is a change-conscious, change-seeking mode of management it is not surprising that one of the primary changes it requires is a change on the part of managers themselves—a change from a traditional mind-set to a new and different one, a new way of thinking about the functioning of the business enterprise, and a reexamination of its purpose and responsibility.

MISSION

- A mission describes the fundamental purpose of an organization, often with the explicit or implicit implication of making an important contribution to the economy, to society, or to human advancement and well-being.

- Companies whose sole purpose is to earn money, or simply to stay in business for the sake of staying in business, are companies that do not have a mission. Any attempt by these companies to write "a mission statement" will have no meaning.

- However, organizations that do have a mission should put the mission in writing, communicate it thoroughly throughout the organization, and make sure it is discussed and understood.

- The effective communication of the mission is absolutely necessary if TQM is to work, since TQM requires a profound sense of purpose on the part of everyone.

MODEL B MANAGEMENT

- TQM is one expression or manifestation of what is being called "The New Management." Over recent decades we have seen more and more instances of the "Old Management" dropping out of use as the New Management replaces it.

- In my own writing, consulting, and teaching, I had come to use the neutral terms, "Model A Management" and "Model B Management."

- The New Management is based on different values and a different world view. In any case it is important for companies to realize that TQM is a part of the New Management and that TQM just doesn't function if force-fit into the traditional paradigm.

- My own interpretation of the old and the new management paradigms is shown in the diagram below. There are, it's worth noting, six different dimensions along which the two differ.

Two Management Paradigms	
The Old	**The New**
Model A	**Model B**
Inward Looking	Outward Looking
Backward Looking	Forward Looking
Authoritarian	Participatory
Habit Driven	Thought Driven
Change Resisting	Change Making
Conventional/Conservative	Innovative/Entrepreneurial

- This six-dimensional model that I began developing twenty years ago highlights the fundamental attributes of the new management that a new society, a new economy, and a whole new world requires.

- Using a survey questionnaire called "The Management Progress Profile" based on the Model A-Model B distinction, my firm has been tracking management change for two decades using an informal approach in which clients have served as voluntary guinea pigs. Two things have stood out in our findings.

  ➤ First, almost all organizations have shown a slow but steady trend from A to B.

  ➤ Second, in every case where a company has made a real jump from A to B, it has been because of a deliberate, conscious, and planned decision to do so. The greatest stimulus to make this jump during the last five years has been the increasing evidence that TQM, one of the manifestations and examples of Model B, is the only paradigm that is proving successful in the new global, competitive world of high-velocity hyper-change, turbulence, and transformation.

MOMENTS OF TRUTH

- *Moments of truth* are those special kinds of events and interactions with customers, some direct and some indirect, that can deeply affect how the customer will feel about the quality of a product or service, and how he or she will perceive the person or the company that is providing it.

- The concept of moments of truth was formulated by Jan Carlzon as president and CEO of Scandinavian Airlines System, and became a key factor in helping that company become a leader in customer service and satisfaction. It's a powerful idea that many other firms have been able to use to their great benefit, and the benefit of their customers. Never underestimate the power of a great idea. Any company can get a great deal of mileage by adopting and using this one.

- One moment of truth might be when the customer contacts a supplier about an overcharge. Or the moment when the customer opens the box and starts reading the software manual. Or the first time that a student (a customer) asks the professor (a supplier) a question, and experiences the professor's tone of response.

- In most businesses, it is possible to single out and identify what some of these moments of truth are, and then to do the utmost to make sure—by planning and training and whatever other means are appropriate—that the experiences the customer will have at these times will be well perceived. In many leading-edge TQM companies, that is exactly what is done.

OPPOSITES

- What makes TQM such a powerful paradigm is its unique ability to reconcile opposites, and turn them into a source of strength.

- Firms that don't understand—whether explicitly or intuitively—this "opposites" characteristic of TQM have difficulty getting the hang of the TQM paradigm.

- TQM brings the *top* and the *bottom* of the organization into a dynamic unity by formulating and communicating a common vision, common values, and common goals.

- TQM bends over backwards to relate the efforts of the *producer* to the needs and wants of *consumers*.

- It takes steps to integrate and harmonize the efforts of the *supplier* with the requirements of the *producer*.

- It integrates the efforts of the *employers* and the *employed* by focusing their attention on a single target: the customer.

- It changes *outsiders and strangers* (salespersons, consultants, visitors, etc.) into *insiders and friends*.

- It strives for both frequent *small improvements* and occasional *large leaps*.

- Through the use of strategic thinking and creative innovation, it uses the *present* as an opportune time to visualize, plan, create, and invent a new corporate *future* different from the *past*.

- It employs special techniques through which *higher quality* products and services are produced at *lower cost*.

- It combines a respect for *facts and data* with an admiration for *the imaginative and the creative*.

- It places an equal value on both *thinking and doing,* and believes they should be joined together.

- It combines the principles of *individualism and competition* with those of *cooperation and teamwork,* with no loss of either.

- More examples of the opposites that are combined, integrated and synthesized in TQM are found throughout this handbook. Inescapably, come to think of it, that's what the handbook is mostly about!

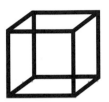

- It is possible to get into the habit of looking at the opposite of anything so that it becomes gradually more instinctive to do so. Have a go at forcing your mind to make the cube shown above slant up or slant down as you want it to.

ORGANIZATIONS AND ASSOCIATIONS

- Most countries today have a number of associations dedicated to the improvement of quality, some of which are nationwide in scope. The associations often supply their members with research, policy advice, training, consulting services, and publications.

- The largest such organization in the world is the American Society for Quality Control, which geographically embraces both the U.S. and Canada.

- Other U.S. organizations include the American Productivity & Quality Center, the Association of American Quality Consultants, and The Center for Quality Management.

- Canadian examples include the Canadian Quality Management Institute, the University of Toronto Institute of Customer-Driven Quality, and Ecole Polytechnique's Association Quebecoise de la Qualite.

- Mexico possesses La Fundacion Mexicana para la Calidad Total.

- Europe has a multinational European Foundation for Quality Management.

OUTWARD-LOOKING COMPANIES

- A true TQM company is not concerned only with what is going on inside itself—inside its offices, plants, and laboratories. It slants much of its attention toward what is going on in the outside world, in the lives and families of its customers, in the world of its suppliers, the community and its institutions, in the government, and so on. That's where the new markets are. Outside. They've been called "the markets of change."

- In the past, many companies tended to be highly absorbed in themselves and their own industry. They were inward-looking and self-centered. But the world's new realities necessitate a profound shift toward greater interest in the outside. Free trade and high-speed communication and transportation can cause new opportunities to spring up from almost anywhere. And they do. So do new threats.

- The new threats and opportunities can come from developments in technologies or sectors of society that once seemed remote from the company or the industry. And they can come with blinding speed.

- When managed in the new outward-looking manner, a TQM company is a company (or school, or hospital, or whatever) that has made this difficult shift of primary attention and interest. It does not regard quality management as a simple matter of improving present products, services, and processes. Far from it.

- The pronounced shift toward this outer orientation is accompanied by *observable changes in behavior and action,* and in the observable proportion of time spent inside the firm and the industry to time spent outside.

- Today's outward-looking firms, scan the environment to detect changes in foreign economies, in their competitors, in their customers, in their suppliers, in technologies, in demographics, in life styles and occupations, in legislation, and in other matters. They monitor trends. They're ready for surprises and ready to respond. They are not change resistant but change responsive. They look for change, they want change, they make change happen.

PARALLEL ORGANIZATION

- The TQM organization presents the image of a beehive of proactive activity in which individuals are not only energetically doing their normal individual jobs but also participating several hours a week in various improvement teams, project teams, innovation teams, or task forces.

- The sum of these TQM improvement teams and groups has been described as a parallel organization because it exists side-by-side with the day-to-day functional organization.

- The patterning of all these small groups or teams is not random. It is structured at any time by the direction and focus of the whole TQM strategy of the firm.

- Collectively, they constitute a network that overlays and overlaps the basic departmental structures.

- They create something that resembles a cobweb that extends well beyond the normal vertical and horizontal boundaries of functions and responsibilities.

- This cobweb or network does not have a permanent overall structure but rather a shape that constantly changes as teams and groups complete a task, and as new teams and groups are constituted to begin new tasks.

- The point, however, is that in the TQM company the existence of two parallel organizations—the functional one and the TQM one—is a new and permanent part of the corporate reality.

PERCEPTION

- Quality has two dimensions: the objective and the subjective.

- The objective dimension is measured in terms of the characteristics of the product or service itself, such features (depending on what we are talking about) as durability, color, strength, purity, thoroughness, freedom from defects, promptness, accuracy, and so on.

- Objective properties are usually easily measurable and highly controllable—and this measurability and controllability provides, to many people, a deep satisfaction. Measurability and controllability have permitted the Japanese, and, increasingly, others to produce impeccable products and deliver services that are sometimes equally impeccable.

- On the other hand, every product and service has its subjective and very human properties: some people love the shape of the Ford Taurus; others loathe it. The Volkswagen Beetle was loved by some for its reliability and economy and rejected by others for its ugliness.

- The same cool austerity in line and shape that causes one person to admire a particular building will give another person the chills.

- One patient may like Dr. X because of his warm, easy-going approach and story-telling and the other patient prefers a doctor who is cool, methodical, quick, and precise. In objective terms, the fact that both doctors are equally good from a technical point of view is an entirely different matter.

- In general, the subjective and the human aspects are more important in services than in products (a good hammer is simply a good hammer but a good meal depends on the company as much as the food).

- Much of our attitude toward quality remains a hold-over from the industrial era when the purely objective, engineering-type of mentality held dominion. For example, some banks think that the quality of customer service is a strict function of such objective features as promptness and convenience, etc. Research, however, has established over and over again that customers take these objective attributes for granted and that they will stay with or leave a bank mainly on the basis of whether they feel they are treated in a friendly and a very helpful fashion, in particular.

- Getting in tune with the service industry era means getting in tune with the subjective needs, wants, feelings, and perceptions of the customer (and the employee, and the supplier, and the person in the next department, and so on.) See MCL GRID for more on measuring customer's subjective responses.

- Consider the following widely used diagram. The conventional expectation is that we should see either an old woman or a young woman. However, those who look with fresh eyes and an open mind see many other things as well: the right shoulder of a gorilla who is writing something on a wall; a penguin; the rear end and shoulders of a naked discus thrower; a porcupine; the right side of the face of a cartoon cave-man; the black head and beak of a vulture; a peeled banana; a distorted smiling face. Ask someone else if they can see the things that you can't.

PERFECTION

- That level of excellence and quality beyond which it is impossible to go, and which in practice is impossible to get to.

- While perfection is an ideal that is never completely attainable, it nonetheless serves as a goal that can be aimed at and, in some fields, very closely approached.

- Perfection can be most closely achieved in physical matters, i.e. with the proper instruments a near-perfect circle can be drawn, some gymnasts and divers achieve almost flawless levels of skill and grace, and some airlines achieve a near-perfect safety performance. (For more, see ZERO DEFECTS.) When the search for perfection becomes a dominant character trait of an individual, it is labeled "perfectionism," and the person, a "perfectionist."

- When carried too far perfectionism becomes a burden to the individual and often to those close to that person. It can, and frequently does, lead to obsessive-compulsive behavior in which the smallest detail, and the most unimportant thing, is never to be over-looked, and where the fear of error and imperfection reaches a neurotic level.

- Perfectionism is one of the potential dangers in TQM—one of those common cases of carrying a good thing too far. A form of extremism.

- A particular danger of perfectionism is that it can inhibit the spontaneity and risk-taking that are essential to creativity, innovation, and entrepreneurship.

PREVENTION VERSUS DETECTION

- Prevention is the process of avoiding errors, defects, etc. before they happen, rather than detecting whether the product, service, or process contains errors, defects, or other quality deficiencies after they have already occurred.

- The guiding maxim under prevention is: "Do it right the first time!"

PROBLEM-SOLVING TOOLS

- At the level of operating detail, TQM makes use of a number of "tools" and "techniques" in the form of graphs, charts, statistical displays, flow diagrams, and the like.

- Techniques and tools are instruments used to achieve the desired goals of TQM. How many of these tools will be useful, and which ones, depends on the nature of the business and the business function being considered. Examples are:

  ➤ The cause-and-effect diagram shows the relationship between an effect and its possible causes. It is sometimes called a fishbone diagram.

  ➤ The histogram is a type of bar graph that shows how measured data is distributed; it thus displays the variations that occur in a process.

  ➤ The control chart plots performance, and tells you whether a process is stable or not. It tells you when to take corrective action and when to keep your hands off.

  ➤ The run chart plots data in such a way as to reveal broad trends and/or variations over time.

  ➤ Scatter diagrams help show the relationship between one variable and another, such as hours of the day and sales calls.

  ➤ Methods for experimental design, such as Taguchi and others of a more advanced form, are techniques for analyzing data in ways that permit analyzing the effect of simultaneous variation of different factors related to a design or manufacturing process; they are useful in optimizing performance.

- More information on these tools can be obtained from the substantial literature that is readily available. For example, an excellent source is a pocket-sized booklet called *The Memory Jogger,* published by GOAL/QPC.

PROCESS CONTROL

- Process control refers to the managing of any process by the people who are performing it by monitoring variance outside established "control limits."

- The process may be managerial, administrative, clerical, production, sales, or service.

PROCESS IMPROVEMENT

- Process improvement may also be referred to as "process re-engineering."

- A process is any series of tasks or activities carried out in the design, development, production, distribution, or sales of a product or service. Processes also include those of a business and management nature such as budgeting, capital appropriation, payroll, financial reporting, recruiting, training, market research, advertising and so on.

- Each step in the process should add value to the original input and be as simple, speedy, and reliable as possible.

- Mapping processes using a flow chart diagram—what is often referred to as "line analysis"—helps in discovering possibilities for improvement.

- Because processes often cross from one departmental boundary to another, cross-departmental teams are usually required for process improvement projects. Many problems in the value-added process chain will occur at these interfaces if responsibilities on either side become blurred.

PRODUCTIVITY

- In the TQM philosophy, the key to successful process and productivity improvement, as well as quality improvement, is the active involvement of the people themselves who do the work.

- Productivity is usually expressed as the ratio between inputs and outputs. Productivity can be expressed as a physical ratio between any input hours, dollars, materials, energy, etc. and any output figure such as weight, numbers, etc. It can also be expressed as the ratio of the financial values concerned.

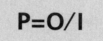

$$P=O/I$$

- Productivity and quality are closely related. An increase in the quality, and hence the value, of a product or a service at no added cost constitutes a productivity gain, i.e. the production of an improved input/output ratio.

- Productivity improvement—often described as producing "more for less"—results from the application of human ingenuity and imagination to the service of finding as many new, different, and better ways of doing things (that is, through making improvements in processes, by finding and using more cost-effective materials, better equipment, or whatever else will do the trick).

- An important benefit from having and making productivity measurements is to be able to compare one's firm with others in the industry. It is not unusual to find one firm whose productivity is half again as great as some others in the same industry. In particular, the opening up of free trade among countries means that more and more firms have to compete not only with firms in their own country but with those in a dozen or more other countries as well. The implications for profits and survivability are obvious.

- Another benefit of productivity measures is to be able to set productivity improvement goals and measure progress in reaching them.

- Among the more important of today's productivity issues are those that have to do with white-collar and clerical productivity in general, and with public sector and government services in particular.

- For a rich reference source, containing over a hundred articles on productivity and quality, take a look at the volume edited by William F. Christopher and Carl G. Thor, titled *Handbook for Productivity Measurement and Improvement.*

PROMETHEAN MANAGEMENT

- Promethean management takes its name from the Greek titan, Prometheus, whose name means "forethought."

- Prometheus stole fire from the gods on Mount Olympus, gave it to mankind, and then taught mankind how to use it.

- Promethean management, therefore, is taken to be management that is forward-looking, future-focused, ambitious, and innovative.

- Prometheus was punished by being chained to a rock where his liver was eaten out by an eagle, a warning to all those bold and ambitious folk who would presume to be too much like the gods. Quite clearly, Promethean management is not a style for the faint of heart.

- At this point, the reader may wish (1) to re-read the definitions of Apollonian and Dionysian management. Then (2) rate yourself from one to ten on where you stand on each of these three godly scales—also, your company.

- It can be taken as a given that high quality in management—all out TQM—presupposes the habitual use of foresight, the presence of vision, and a considerable urge to "invent the future." Otherwise, it just ain't TQM.

PURPOSEFUL MANAGEMENT

- Organizations and persons who have a clear and definite sense of purpose can direct their energies more effectively, act more decisively.

- But consciousness of purpose, intentionality, is something that can easily fade and blur into aimlessness and drift.

- Organizations are originally brought into being to serve some purpose, and for a while will function in a highly purposeful manner. But with the passage of time the original, founding purpose may be lost and with it the organization's viability. A sense of purpose and meaning is as necessary to a satisfactory existence as even such basics as air, food, and water.

- Only purposeful people and purposeful organizations are capable of setting targets for quality and putting energy and dedication into the effort to achieve them. The organization has, therefore, first of all to find or re-discover its sense of purpose before it can set about aiming at excellence. A sense of purpose and dedication will provide everyone with the direction, the will, and the energy that's needed to improve.

- Start with a deep, serious and soul-searching executive retreat. Hold it in a remote location, on a mountain top or at a lakeshore or the seaside, and take two to three days.

- For more information on how to translate the corporate sense of purpose into objectives, action, and results, see the section headed MBOR.

QUALITY

- The quality movement was inspired by the insistent cry from consumers and taxpayers for a considerable improvement in the quality of what they were receiving.

- In TQM, the meaning of "quality" is defined operationally rather than abstractly in terms of what the customer wants, needs, and expects. It is the customer rather than the company who judges the quality of the product or service.

- There can be no single generic definition of quality but only specific definitions worked out for particular kinds of clients and consumers of specific kinds of products or services.

- Quality contains objective and subjective elements. Both the objective and subjective elements will depend on what product or service we are talking about. In some cases, the objective elements may mean having a product or service provided on time, free of defects, and reliable in operation. Subjective elements might mean that it is easy to purchase, pleasant to the eye, comfortable to use, or entertaining to own.

- Quality is a concept that has a universal application. Everything can be measured in terms of its degree of quality. The concept of quality was first applied to products, then to the service associated with the product, then to services as such, then to the quality of processes (such as a manufacturing or an accounting process), and finally to the quality of everything important in a business—the quality of leadership, the quality of management, the quality of research, the quality of training, the quality of work-life, the quality of a company's ethics, and so on.

- The force behind quality is a drive for excellence. The drive for excellence will not satisfy itself with quality only in some areas but seeks quality in all. That's what the *total* in *total quality management* means.

QUALITY ACTION TEAMS

- A quality action team is a small group of six or seven employees who work together on one or another improvement opportunity.

- Sometimes, however, an action team may include a customer, a supplier, or some other person or persons who are needed for their contributions.

- The opportunity to be tackled may be a process improvement, a product or service improvement, a customer service improvement, or any other improvement that is to the benefit of one or all the company's stakeholders. (See STAKEHOLDER.)

- Members of a quality action team have all been trained in team leadership, team management, team membership, and in the various analytical and creative tools that are used in TQM.

- The team tries to formulate its goal and objective as clearly as possible, and sets up a schedule of meetings (extending often over a several week period).

- The team is often aided in its initial performance by the presence of a "facilitator," a person who has skills in group dynamics and TQM and is able to help the team learn how to function effectively.

QUALITY ASSURANCE

- Quality assurance means to assure quality in a product or service so that a customer can purchase it with confidence and experience satisfaction.

- Canadian quality consultant John Prior sees "assurance" as refer-
ring to the actions necessary to *make certain* that quality objectives are met.

- Before the advent of TQM, quality assurance referred to the Quality Assurance Departments that inspected output to sort out any
defects for rework or discard. In the era of TQM, however, we
prevent defects before they happen, and this is not done by a
Quality Assurance Department but by employees working in
quality teams.

- My colleague Bill Christopher, president of the Management
Innovations Group in Connecticut, explains that *"quality assurance has changed its meaning."* It now means, he says, *"...doing all
those things that we wrap into the TQM package."*

- In today's environment quality assurance is regarded as more
important than ever, and the idea is spreading. For example,
Ontario hospitals, to be accredited, have to have quality assurance programs. In this context, quality assurance can be defined
as: *"The establishment of hospital-wide goals, the assessment of the procedures in place to see if they achieve these goals, and, if not, the pro-
posal of solutions to achieve these goals."* (Canadian Council on Hospital Accreditation, 1985.) It is presumed that hospitals will
achieve their quality goals by adopting the TQM management
paradigm. (Because of their authoritarian traditions, hospitals
face a bigger challenge than most other sectors in moving toward
the empowerment and total involvement of employees that is at
the heart of TQM.)

- Again, for example, many firms, particularly multinationals, are
adopting ISO 9000 international standards as a means of assur-
ing customers that processes have been put into place that will
assure quality. Some purchasers require such an assurance from
their suppliers as a condition of entering into a contract.

QUALITY CIRCLES

- The "circle" refers to a small face-to-face group, usually of ten or fewer members, employees and/or managers, who get together at frequent intervals to work out solutions to quality, service, cycle time, and productivity issues.

- Names other than "quality circle," but which have a similar meaning, are also used, e.g., "work group," "quality team," and "improvement team," among others.

- The trend is for companies to invent their own names.

QUALITY CONTROL

- Quality control is the process of monitoring a product, service, or process; comparing the degree to which it conforms or deviates from an established standard of quality; and taking corrective action to prevent future unacceptable variations from the standard that has been set. (See PROBLEM SOLVING for descriptions of some of the seven QC tools.)

QUALITY FUNCTION DEPLOYMENT

- QFD is a set of planning and communication routines for product development that insures customer needs are built into new design specifications.

- It uses a basic conceptual tool known as a *house of quality*, which is a multidimensional grid or matrix.

- The purpose of QFD is to enable marketing, design, and production to work together from the very beginning of a new product idea in order to make sure it meets the customer's expectations and requirements.

- QFD originated in 1972 in Mitsubishi's Kobe shipyard site.

- An excellent article on QFD titled "The House of Quality," by John R. Hauser and Don Clausing, is to be found in *Harvard Business Review*, May-June 1988. See also *Quality Function Deployment* by Yoji Akao.

QUALITY MANAGEMENT

- Quality management has two different but complementary meanings: *the quality of management and the management of quality.*

- Only firms that have an exceptionally high quality of management will have any real success in managing quality.

- Many firms don't have the managerial moxie and the people skills it takes. Therefore many attempts at TQM are destined to fail before they begin.

- Afterwards, however, the blame is often placed on TQM itself—"A good idea but it doesn't work," we may hear them say.

Quality Management means	1. The management of quality 2. The quality of management

- The term *quality of management* can be taken to mean the quality of vision, imagination, foresight and leadership, the quality of strategic thinking and action, the quality of organization and communication, the quality of management training and development, the intelligence of decision-making, the caliber of management entrepreneurship and innovativeness, and a host of other aspects of the management process too numerous to specify.

- There is an increasing recognition that because of global competition, the quality of management in any given country or company must be as good as or better than that of other countries and companies. This leads to the conclusion that continuous improvement in the quality and excellence of a company's managers and its management processes is an absolute necessity.

- The management paradigm that is needed for survival in a world of discontinuous and disorderly change must be different from the traditional, conservative, hierarchical, habit-driven, inward-looking, change-resistant, authoritarian model of the last five (and more) decades. What has been emerging has been described as the "new management" in contrast with the "old." TQM plainly falls within the new paradigm. It can't work outside of it.

- Our own version of the new management describes it as having a number of quite clearly identifiable features:

  ➤ future-focused
  ➤ outward-oriented
  ➤ participatory
  ➤ idea-driven
  ➤ change-responsive
  ➤ innovative
  ➤ entrepreneurial

- The term *management of quality* can be taken to mean the unembarrassed employment of a high-minded new people-centered business and management paradigm. Its aim is excellence: the imaginative and strategic utilization of resources, processes, and equipment—in such a way as to deliver continuously improving and ever-innovative new value to customers, employees, society, and shareholders, at ever decreasing cost, and to the greatest benefit of the economy and the country.

QUALITY OF LIFE

- The quality of human life depends not only on economic well-being but on other equally important factors as well. These other factors include physical and mental health, the social order, social institutions (medicine, justice, education) political stability, and the environment.

- In some "advanced industrial societies," a decline in safety on the streets—or even in the home—is registering high on the scale of quality of life concerns. Societies that perform at high economic and technological levels may perform at low levels with regard to some of the things that make life most worth living. This contradiction arises out of the values that dominate or don't dominate in the culture of the society in question. Understanding such socioeconomic contradictions is complicated by the even more subtle contradiction that exists when the values that are publicly expressed and extolled in any society may be the exact opposite of those which actually drive the behavior of its people and institutions.

- Nobody ever said that human beings, their societies, and their institutions are easy to understand. In "advanced" societies, physical, sexual, and emotional abuse at the hands of professionals, law-enforcers, government officials, doctors, teachers, parents, and spouses appears to be commonplace.

- There is an increasing expectation that executives and managers must go beyond their traditional managerial roles, and narrower corporate obligations, and exercise leadership in helping society find ways and means to moderate some of these more common blights on the quality of life.

- Various social and economic "indicators" have been developed and employed for the purpose of making international comparisons of the quality of life in different societies. In 1992, The Human Development Report, published by the United Nations Development Programme, ranked Canada as the No. 1 country in the world for quality of life. The criteria are life expectancy, education levels, and purchasing power. One hundred and sixty countries were compared. Yet anyone who knows anything about Canadian realities would not conclude that a No. 1 ranking implies that the country lacks a considerable collection of sorrows and horrors. Continuous improvement, steadily pursued, is the only thing that holds out the hope for a better future for all countries, wherever they may be on the scale.

- Significant discoveries have recently been through research that has been done on the important causal relationship between the quality of the social health of a community and the quality and performance of its economy. It appears that the economic health and prosperity of a country is made possible when there is an underlying good quality in the social, institutional, and human relationships that exist in that country. When the social fabric of a nation is in disrepair and is poor in quality, high levels of economic growth and productivity cannot be successfully attained.

- Improving the quality level of social institutions and human relationships can help a city, a region, or a state become more prosperous. For example, it is often remarked that the impressive economic achievements of South Carolina are partly due to that state's careful nurturing of its educational institutions and the way in which this attracts new companies.

QUALITY OF TIME

- Quality time is time that is spent in pleasant, enjoyable, enriching, and high payoff activities, as against time spent in discomfort, pain, boredom, and in routine, or unrewarding, low payoff (and even pointless and wasteful) activities, whether on or off the job.

- TQM organizations analyze and observe what people at work spend their time doing, what the quality of that time is, and how things can be re-organized to increase the amount of time that is high quality and reduce the amount that is low.

- Persons interested in improving the quality of their lives pay attention to what they spend their time doing—and who they spend their time with. As Benjamin Franklin put it, *"Dost thou love life? Then do not squander time; for that's the stuff life is made of."*

QUALITY OF WORKING LIFE

- The quality of life experienced on and off the job can be measured by such indices as health and safety, respect and dignity, congenial working relationships, equality of opportunity, job challenge and richness, freedom to think critically and creatively, freedom of expression, and opportunities for learning, growth, and development.

- TQM business enterprises include this domain of quality in their sights, and try to make life better for their employees. In 1992, IBM and eleven other major corporations (including AT&T, Kodak, American Express, Exxon) inaugurated programs to help employees care for their children or elderly parents.

QUALITIVITY

- A hybrid term that combines the two words, quality and productivity, to express the idea that TQM firms are concerned with both. In TQM firms, huge gains in productivity often occur as a result of the application of process improvement methods.

QUANTUM LEAPS

- A quantum leap is the large and abrupt kind of advance that takes place when, instead of improving something that already exists, something new is brought into existence.

- Historical examples of quantum leaps include penicillin, jet airplanes, driverless trains, the quartz watch, parallel processing, organ transplants, matrix organizations, employee empowerment, team management, statistical process control, just-in-time production, activity accounting, and zero-based budgeting.

- When major breakthroughs such as these are made, the innovating company or individual obtains a major and profound advantage. In some cases, as in instant photography and xerography, whole new industries are created.

- A quantum leap is a form of qualitative change rather than quantitative change. It represents a breaking away from an established pattern and the opening up of possibilities that are both new and different.

- Such breakthroughs are achieved by people who are in the habit of employing deep processes of mental paradigm-shifting, concept re-examination, thought expansion, and other powerful forms of creative and imaginative thinking.

- One of the major challenges to TQM is how to encourage both continuous improvements and discontinuous breakthroughs.

- Tensions of conviction and persoality often exist between those who favor steady improvement and incrementalism and those who favor innovation, breakthroughs, and quantum leaps.

ROLE

- One's role is the part played, or the function performed, in carrying out a mission, working toward some purpose, and accomplishing some useful results in the process.

- Common roles in society are those of teacher, policeman, nurse, doctor, etc.

- In some TQM organizations brief and simple statements of job "role" are replacing the traditional and lengthier job "descriptions." The role explains only mission, purpose, and expected results; the description explains in more or less detail what activities are to be engaged in.

- The job role concept encourages managers and employees to focus more clearly on the mission to be accomplished and the results to be achieved. It allows the specific activities to be worked out by the job-holder. There is no single best way of doing any job. The person doing the job is the best one to determine what activities are required. Circumstances and situations will be encountered where it is best if the job-holder use personal judgment and initiative. Most of today's businesses are too fast-moving and flowing to be frozen into the fixed form provided by traditional job descriptions.

- A valuable by-product of the change from job description to job role is a reduction in the very considerable cost and paperwork associated with the tradition of detailed job descriptions.

Scientific Method

- An important part of the power of TQM arises from its conscious and deliberate use of scientific method.

- Fundamental to the method is an emphasis on obtaining *facts and data* as a basis for judgment, planning and decision-making. Often called "fact-based management," or "data-driven decision-making." For example, in establishing quality standards for customer satisfaction, full in-depth intensive surveys and questionnaires will be employed and the data rigorously analyzed. Conjecture and speculation about customer expectations, requirements, and satisfaction are thus replaced by fact and measurement.

- Data is gathered on cycle time, process time, errors, defects, delays, waste, and other aspects of quality performance and measurements, and comparisons are made between the actual and the desired.

- In these respects, TQM is serving to bring about a renaissance in traditional principles of "scientific management."

Searching

- Searching is an activity that TQM managers and employees engage in constantly—day in and day out.

- The search is a double one—a search into the firm's market environment and a search into the interior of the firm itself.

- There is incessant first-hand, *personal* investigation of the business environment for new revenue opportunities and possibilities from new customers, new markets, and new human or societal needs.

- This search may include many people in addition to the person in question, yet the person still engages in it himself or herself. It's not something to delegate mainly or entirely to others.

- Searching is most certainly not merely the technocratic, bookish poring through data and statistics that the pedantic "analyst" wants it to be. It's a real search, a physical search, carried by foot, and car, and plane—often, these days, extending into foreign places. It's the kind of searching explorers do. A search with eyes and ears open. A search that takes energy and muscle and that uses all five senses. An entrepreneurial rather than a scholarly venture! Or should we say adventure?

- The seeker is always hot on the trail of new opportunities and possibilities, of important things that are waiting to be discovered. It's the entrepreneur's quest.

- There is an endless search, internally as well, for better ways to improve products, services and processes, reduce costs and waste, increase productivity, so that all the stakeholders needs and expectations can be better met. Searching takes effort and it takes skill. It calls upon a greater use of our human resources. There is an ancient saying that there are *"those who have eyes and cannot see, who have ears and cannot hear."*

- Let's face it. Sometimes—in fact often—we don't see what's right in front of our eyes. Look at the diagram below for example. What do you see?

- Most of us do not see that the word *the* appears twice! We are seeing what we expect to see, rather than what's really there.

- The moral is that we are always approaching the world with built-in preconceptions and expectations that stop us from seeing things clearly and fully. In a changing world, our expectations are always falling behind the actual facts. What we have to do is look at lot more carefully than we sometimes do.

- Searching—using our eyes and ears—is most definitely a skill that takes effort, but it's one that we can all learn, and it is a skill that grows with practice. Searching is also a game that is fun and rewarding. The game of business.

- Company after company has demonstrated what can happen when they turn to energetic searching. New opportunities and possibilities are always discovered. Costs may go down, sales may go up, and profits and employment security may increase.

SELF-MANAGEMENT

- Under advanced TQM concepts, every employee becomes a manager of his or her own area of responsibility and is taught how to use the management process.

- Individual employees use management by objectives methods to manage themselves instead of being managed by a boss or supervisor.

- They work within the framework of corporate and departmental objectives with the mission of delivering value to the customer.

- The traditional concepts of hierarchy are profoundly altered.

- The boss becomes a leader, guide, coach, and assistant.

SERENDIPITY

- General Mills paid a small Florida baker over a million of today's dollars for his invention of brown-and-serve rolls, an invention he made entirely by accident. The man happened to be a volunteer fireman. Twenty minutes after he had placed rolls in an oven, the fire alarm sounded. He took them out of the oven and went out to the fire. Three hours later, he rebaked them instead of throwing them out, which he might well have done. Presto, brown-and-serve. This process of accidental discovery or invention, of good luck, is referred to as serendipity.

- Serendipity is more common in business than is generally recognized, or in life itself, for that matter. The plain truth is many good things, as well as bad, happen by accident, by chance.

- As another example, one paper company discovered an opportunity to do business in Brazil as a result of a conversation a senior executive just happened into during some purposeless small talk.

- The stick-on notes that 3M has had so much success with—they've become a basic part of today's office—were the result of a serendipitous accident. 3M had inadvertently produced a glue that would stick but not stick strongly enough. An "unglue," someone has called it. Perfect for little stick-on notes.

- Fleming discovered penicillin when the window of a lab was accidentally left open and penicillin mold drifted in at night and killed the bacteria in a petri dish.

- George Westinghouse discovered the power of pneumatics while reading a Boy Scout magazine that explained how pneumatic drills worked. The idea of the airbrake immediately leapt to his mind. (Westinghouse happened to be active in Baden-Powell's Boy Scout movement.)

- One day, James Schlatter of G. D. Searle & Co. was trying to mix some amino acids to come up with a test for an ulcer drug. Some of it got on his fingers and when he licked it off it tasted sweet. That's how he discovered the artificial sweetener aspartame! Within three years aspartame was accounting for 70 percent of the company's profits. And for another researcher, the discovery of the sweetener, sodium cyclamate, came just as fortuitously. Michael Sveda, a graduate student in chemistry at the University of Illinois, was trying out various compounds in an effort to find one that would reduce fevers. He accidentally got one of the compounds onto his lips. It tasted sweet. It was sodium cyclamate.

- One could easily fill an encyclopedia-length book with examples of serendipitous discoveries. They may well be the rule rather than the exception.

- The word *serendipity* was coined by Horace Walpole, after a fairy tale called *The Three Princes of Serendip*. In this tale, it seems three princes were sent out by their father to travel the world for a year with no plan in mind. During the year, they fell across all kinds of marvels, adventures, and prizes.

- Most people can trace the job that they hold back to some unrelated and unplanned event that lead to their meeting with their present employer; similarly with the matter of how they first came to meet the spouse they are now living with. Try it on yourself. If you think back over your life, you'll realize that the most important things were often those that happened adventitiously rather than by intention or plan. Since this has been so in the past, you can conclude that it will continue to be so for the rest of your life as well. Chances are fair that something unplanned will happen within the next year or two that will alter the direction of your life in a significant way. One can say the same of your company. That's the way the universe of events unfolds, part by plan and part by accident.

- Good luck and serendipity happen most often to those people who are doing the most in the first place. Having discovered that it happens, they tend to be on the alert for more of it, and actively look for it. Good luck also happens most to those who like to stray off the beaten paths and go down the most unfamiliar by-ways.

- Innovative, entrepreneurial style firms are by nature forward-looking and outward-looking, and ever on the alert for the unanticipated and the unexpected. They love to be surprised. (Old-type firms often prided themselves on the fact that they were guided by the rule of—can you believe it ?—"No surprises"!)

- TQM firms form *Opportunity Search* teams who get out of their offices and plants and travel outside their company—and outside their industry. They explore the market environment for new possibilities, things waiting to be found.

- They form *Innovation Teams* and *Venture Teams* inside the company, knowing with certainty that the innovation teams will accidentally discover some product and process enhancement possibilities.

- Earlier forms of management did not take serendipity into account. They were wholly control-oriented, were devoted to a total faith in the power of knowledge and analysis. They saw the random, the fortuitous, the coincidental, or the accidental in negative rather than positive terms.

- Modern-day managers (like modern-day sub-atomic physicists) know that the world operates on the simultaneous principle of both order and disorder, on both determinism and randomness, on both the intentional and the accidental. They believe in both hard work and good luck, in both chance and lawfulness. *They deliberately work both sides of the order-disorder street.*

- Serendipity can, paradoxically, be made to happen. Go for it. Stir up the dust, and it'll happen. Serendipity is more frequent in today's disordered and chaotic world than ever before in human history. Be ready for it. As someone once put it, I think it was Pasteur, "Chance favors the prepared mind."

SHEWHART CYCLE

- This is better known as "PDCA" or "plan-do-check-act."

- It represents four steps used in many improvement strategies.

- PDCA was developed by Walter A. Shewhart, a statistician in Bell Labs in the twenties and thirties.

- Shewhart also pioneered the use of statistical tools to monitor, measure, and control variations in quality.

- He also pioneered the use of "control" charts as part of his process.

- The PDCA cycle is also known as the Deming cycle because of his advocacy of it.

- Basically it is a restatement of the "management process" that was first described at the turn of the century by the French industrialist, Henri Fayol. Fayol discovered that successful firms employed a deliberate process of planning, organization, implementation, and control. Firms that went bankrupt did not. Fayol's discovery of the existence of the management process was, without question, one of the great discoveries of all time, and it gave rise to the possibility of training people how to use it, and for making it a foundation for corporate proficiency.

- GM, under Alfred Sloan, used the management process in 1921 to save GM from bankruptcy and turn the company into the largest in the world. GM calls its version of the management process "The GM Management System." GE, under Ralph Cordiner, called it the "GE Management Philosophy," and used it to turn GE around in 1950. (That GM was to sink eventually into a condition of elephantine torpor should not be allowed to obscure its once great glory.) The American Management Association for decades taught that Fayol's management process spelled the difference between success and failure, and between the management amateur and the management pro.

- The main idea is that if you want to be effective and successful in anything you do, you are well advised to plan, organize, act, observe results, re-adjust, and re-plan.

- In some school systems children are now being taught to apply it to their schoolwork. It will stay with them forever!

- In TQM companies its use is taught to grassroots employees in order to enable them to be self-managing.

- It is important to emphatically note that quality management includes the word management. The implication is that we must *consciously employ the management process* if we are ever to achieve outstanding levels of quality.

SILOS

- A vertically constructed tower with hardened walls used to either store grain or house military missiles.

- In TQM lingo, silos are the vertically organized functional departments such as accounting, purchasing, human resources, engineering, production, sales, and the like. Some companies use the term "chimneys" or "stovepipes" to convey the same idea.

- TQM uses multidisciplinary teams to break through the walls of the corporate silo system and to manage and improve the lateral flow of the work and processes necessary to design, make, and deliver products and services to the customer.

SOCIAL RESPONSIBILITY

- A TQM company is a socially responsible company that is actively concerned and involved with the improvement and protection of the environment, the integrity and quality of its products and services, the honesty and truth of its advertising, the quality and welfare of its community and its country, and the general good of society. It views society as one of its stakeholders.

STAKEHOLDER

....

- A stakeholder group is any group that has a vested interest in the survival and success of a business enterprise, or of any other organization.

- Stakeholders rights are increasingly being written into the law and are receiving increasing legal protection. Legislation already exists in over twenty-five U.S. states, ordaining that a corporation's board of directors has a responsibility to all stakeholders.

- The stakeholder group could include:

➤ owners	➤ suppliers
➤ directors	➤ minorities
➤ managers	➤ the community
➤ employees	➤ the government
➤ customers	

- TQM managers accept the responsibility of concerning themselves with the rights—and the responsibilities—of the various stakeholder groups.

Partners and Stakeholders

Owners | Customers | Suppliers | The Win/Win Philosophy | Managers | Community | Employees

- Research is showing that keeping the interests of all the stakeholders firmly in mind pays off in better bottom-line performance for the enterprise. Professors Max Clarkson, Michael C. Deck, and their colleagues at the Center for Corporate Social Performance and Ethics at the University of Toronto reported that

  ...in order to achieve average or above average profits in its industry, a corporation must manage its stakeholder relationships in order to satisfy the needs and expectations of its principal stakeholder groups on a continuing basis. Without such balanced performance the data showed that corporations did not achieve above-average profits in their industries.

STATISTICAL PROCESS CONTROL

- A method of monitoring, measuring, analyzing and reducing variations in quality of products and services.

- Identifies and controls the extent to which they fall within a range acceptable to the customer.

STRATEGIC DECISION MAKING

- Examining the total set of all possibilities and alternatives put forward during the strategic thinking process.

- Weighing the risks and the rewards, and making the final selection of new courses of action to be implemented.

STRATEGIC MANAGEMENT

- Strategic management is a form of management that proceeds through the formulation and implementation of strategies. (See the section in this handbook entitled STRATEGIC THINKING.)

- In a TQM enterprise, great importance is attached to having high quality strategies, and executives who are excellent strategists.

- Ideally, strategy dictates everything. In particular, the form and structure of the organization in a strategically managed enterprise will be that which is best suited to carrying out strategy.

- In a strategically managed enterprise, all activities such as training, quality assurance, or advertising exist only as tools to enable strategies to be implemented and should be carefully crafted to support the execution of strategy. In firms that are not "strategically managed," such activities are often carried on without regard to whether or not they help execute strategies since, of course, there are no strategies to start with. (For more on this point, see MBOR.)

- Strategic management experts never tire of explaining that having good strategies is not enough. Successful implementation, they emphasize, is crucial.

- In strategic management, provision should be made for monitoring the results, and for the consequent re-evaluation and re-casting of the strategy.

STRATEGIC PLANNING

- Strategic planning includes the processes of strategic thinking and strategic decision-making, plus the additional creative thinking and planning required in order to determine how to successfully implement the strategies successfully.

- *Strategic planning is sometimes mistakenly taken to mean an extension or extrapolation of operational plans in order to cover a longer time frame.*

STRATEGIC PLANNING OF QUALITY

- Companies must plan and develop the way in which quality objectives and programs will be integrated into the firm's overall strategy.

- Having done that, they must then plan and design a program for unfolding the quality improvement process stage by stage into all aspects of the company's life.

- For a look at one way in which a company may plan its approach to quality see HOSHIN MANAGEMENT.

- Whether the planning of quality is done the hoshin way or some other way, the important point is that if quality management is not a well-planned process, it just won't work.

- A neglect to integrate quality goals and programs into the company's strategic objectives constitutes one of the many ways in which attempts at TQM will simply not pan out.

- TQM has to be recognized from the beginning to be one of the most challenging change processes that the company will ever attempt. As well, of course, as one of the most rewarding. The least it will require is good planning.

STRATEGIC THINKING

- Strategic thinking is the kind of creative thinking required of a person or group confronting an uncertain, ambiguous, changing situation when appropriate courses of action are not clear, and when established or routine solutions are insufficient or inappropriate.

- Strategic thinking requires a re-examination of mission, objectives, policies, and solutions, and the imaginative presentation of a spectrum of new alternatives, some of which may have to be created from pure imagination.

- Sometimes it requires a penetrating and difficult examination of basic premises and even of basic beliefs and concepts—in other words a fundamental paradigm shift and a search for new ways of thinking and perceiving reality.

- The quality of strategic thinking employed by a firm is increasingly understood to be a principal measurement of the quality of its leadership.

SUMMING IT UP

- TQM is a mode of management that has been formulated—formally organized—for the purpose of achieving excellence. It is the result of a long process of evolution.

- The more one reads the case studies the more one is impressed with the possibility that something unusual, powerful, and practical may be at work. Quality and excellence are ideals that have a powerful force. The evidence shows that most people are magnetized by it. We will no longer settle for the mediocre or the shoddy, neither in our products nor our institutions. More compelling may be the fear that if we do not pursue excellence, others will.

- It's not hard to discover what TQM is in its formalities and methods. But what is most important is to realize that TQM rests upon a deep structure of human beliefs, insights, and values—some old as the hills and some more recent.

- The list reads like this:

  1. Total quality means quality in every aspect of the business.

  2. Quality adds value.

  3. Quality management means both the quality of management and the management of quality.

4. Total quality management requires a strategic/systemic approach.

5. Quality management supports the stakeholder concept.

6. Quality comes from the striving for excellence.

7. Excellence is achieved through constant improvement.

8. Quality improvement requires constant creativity and innovation.

9. Quality management gives precedence to quality over quantity.

10. Quality management is ethical management.

11. Quality management flourishes best in an environment of permanent change.

12. Quality management rewards risk-taking, enterprise, and innovation.

13. Quality management requires a new form of permeable, tight-loose organization.

14. Quality is defined by the customer and the client.

15. Quality improvement requires creative customer input.

16. Quality management means *employee empowerment and teamwork.*

17. Quality management thrives on self control versus external control.

18. Quality improvement implies a dynamic corporate culture of ceaseless learning and education.

19. Quality and productivity are closely related.

20. Quality management uses techniques but is anything but a technique.

- The nature of this list tells us plainly that TQM will invite us to make a profound change in the culture and climate of our organizations. Its focus is primarily upon people—their courage, their beliefs, their emotions, their energies, and their brains.

- The technocratically inclined who take TQM to be a mere set of methods, procedures, and techniques will be disappointed when it fails for them, and fail it must.

SUPPLIER QUALITY ASSURANCE

- An agreed upon assurance from your supplier that a product or service provided to you will meet your requirements so that you in turn will be able to meet your customer's requirements. (See QUALITY ASSURANCE for more.)

SYNERGY

- *Synergy* is a key factor in success. It means "working together"—*syn* means together, and *erg* means work.

- The word *synergy* was originally invented in the field of medicine after it had been discovered that sometimes drugs that produced no effect when used separately had curative powers when used together—a truly astonishing phenomenon.

- Water is made of hydrogen and oxygen but possesses properties (it dissolves sugar, freezes into ice, can be drunk, etc.) that neither of its two constituents possess. Sulfuric acid contains the same two elements, hydrogen and oxygen, plus sulfur. All three when separate have no power to burn or corrode, but joined in a union as sulfuric acid will go through a sheet of metal in no time at all. As the kids' limerick put it:

  Alas, poor Willie. Willie is no more. For what he thought was H_2O was H_2SO_4.

- In the field of corporate mergers and acquisitions (an activity engaged in by many TQM firms, as well as non-TQM firms), the synergy phenomenon is sometimes accompanied by the remark, "Hey, this is a real two-plus-two-equals-five deal!"

- That the whole could be greater (more profitable, more effective, more beautiful, more whatever) than the mere sum of its parts is one of the miracles of nature—and of business!—that seems to contradict common-sense logic, all the more so because of its impressive truth.

- Synergy is created by the use of teams, by the company-customer partnership, by the supplier-company partnership, by the systems engineering approach which integrates all three into an efficient flow, and in numerous other ways. Small wonder TQM has such bigger-than-life clout!

SYNTROPY

- Synergy is related to syntropy. Syntropy is the tendency for certain things to join together in a creative union and to form wholes that are more than, and different from, the sum of the parts. It is the creative process.

- An example is when a couple forms a family. Then again when the family has children.

- Another syntropic process is when families form a community, and when the resulting communities form a nation.

- Oxygen and hydrogen are so syntropic that when they meet they create an explosion! Energy is released.

- When a supplier and a customer join in a transaction under appropriate circumstances, wealth is created; the supplier has more money than before, and the buyer has more goods or benefits.

- Putting a propeller and an engine on a glider in order to make an airplane. Putting the right musical notes together in the right combination. Putting a steam engine on a trolley to make a train. Putting together the right CEO with the right firm.

- Syntropy represents a patterning of elements into a structure that has order and form.

- Some formal techniques for creative thinking such as morphology, attribute listing, and forced association have the explicit purpose of helping the user to form such new patterns. They help the user to find ways in which things previously uncombined will be combined for the first time, with the result of producing a new invention of a physical, chemical, social, or other nature depending on the field in which the innovative person happens to be working.

- The opposite of syntropy is entropy, the tendency of things to fall apart, to scatter, to lose their pattern! It leads to disorder and formlessness. The energy in the structure peters away. Over the centuries the beautiful building turns to dust. The fresh young beauty fades into a dry and wrinkled elder. The country breaks up into warring factions.

- Information puts order, arrangement, meaning, and energy into a random collection of parts. But then, entropically, the order turns into disorder, the pattern dissipates. The information has gone from the scene. It can neither be recognized nor recovered. It's gone.

- Syntropy is the force of construction just as entropy is the process of destruction. Syntropy, then, is creativity; it produces an ordered structure.

- Syntropy is brought about by information acting upon (informing, if you will) chaos and disorder. It draws upon energy. (Norbert Wiener and others have pointed out that information is "neg-entropy" and the mathematical expression for energy and information are the same.)

- Concepts like syntropy and entropy are part of the necessary understanding of today's executives. They are of very great practical importance. It is essential for leaders of any enterprise to know deeply in their guts that only syntropy, when put to work, can hold the enterprise on a course for survival.

- Since the force of entropy never ceases to do its dirty work, executives must draw always on their resources of energy, courage, and creativity in order to contend with it. Replacing entropy with syntropy is an eternal battle. Courage and creativity, much more than mere logic and analysis, are the hallmarks of executive success in today's world of turmoil and change.

- TQM is a syntropic force that builds and creates, that improves and invents, that brings people and resources together into constructive, higher-valued new patterns and forms.

Systems Thinking

- Systems thinking is a way of looking at how the parts of anything act together to form an effectively functioning whole as against looking at the parts individually and separately. TQM is itself the result of a systems way of thinking. It also calls for a systems way of thinking whenever it's employed.

- What's a system? The human body with its different parts and processes is one example of a system. So is a flower, a tree, a lake, or an entire ecosystem. The whole universe and everything in it is constructed of systems—systems ranging in size and in hierarchical order from the smallest atom to the largest galaxy.

- An automobile is a system, and so is a computer, a computer network, or a robot. Likewise a family, a corporation, or a country.

- A characteristic of living systems is that they keep themselves integrated, directed, and in balance by sub-systems of communication and control. They are self-managing.

- In dynamic systems continuous self-adjustment takes place through information feedback and control. Examples: A human body will automatically develop a tan to protect itself from the sun's rays. A company losing money will almost certainly start to cut back on costs and look for ways of doing more with less (productivity improvement). Many computers nowadays contain certain auto-diagnostic programs that spot problems in the computer and correct them instantaneously.

- Systems thinking takes place when we become conscious of the systems nature of reality and learn to see systems and interconnections everywhere.

- Systems thinking looks at the forest as well as the trees. Systems thinkers always keep in mind the thought that the whole is more than and different from the sum of its parts.

- Systems thinking takes it as axiomatic that getting system patterns and connections right, and making them function effectively, is imperative.

- Systems thinking can lead top management to perceive that the firm is an *open system,* an intimate and interactive part of the larger, dynamically-changing society and economy, a part of the whole, rather than something separate to itself.

- Top managers—those who are systems thinkers—see the business as a complex system whose constituent sub-systems—people, technology, money, management processes—have to mesh together if performance and quality are to be expected.

- Systems thinking means realizing that how well the individual does his/her own job is important but that equally important is how well they integrate their work with that of others.

- Among other things, managers who are systems thinkers attach high value to integration and coordination.

- Leadership is a systems concept. A true leader is an orchestra conductor who helps the corporate players to harmonize.

- Systems thinking means organizing and managing a company in such a way that the different functional departments work together to achieve the firm's goals, not merely to achieve their own departmental objectives.

- It means that a product is holistically designed to high technical standards, in such a way that it is easy and economical to produce, and pleasing to the customer in every way.

TEAMS

- A team is a small face-to-face group whose optimum size is from four or five to nine individuals.

- To function as a team it must have explicit missions, roles, goals, and objectives and be dominated by the desire to perform, achieve, and produce.

- The use of teams at all levels and in all departments of an organization is one of the most outstanding features of leading-edge, high-quality, high-performance organizations. The network of teams to be found operating in such firms is sometimes extensive enough to be referred to as a "parallel organization."

- In particular, the use of cross-departmental teams can integrate and improve the logical flow and quality of value-adding processes involved in the design, production, and delivery of the product or service.

- Teams are variously referred to, depending on purpose or preference, as "management teams," "design teams," "project teams," "quality teams," "quality circles," "productivity teams," "project teams," or "innovation teams."

- Membership in a team should be based on capability to make a contribution rather than on formal position or role.

TEAM LEARNING

- Team learning is also known as *synergogy*, a term coined by Jane Mouton and Robert Blake. The term *synergogy* means "learning together." For a full explication of team-learning, get hold of their book, *Synergogy: A New Strategy for Education, Training, and Development.*

- The point is that TQM is an approach to business management in which teams are used not only to work on specific matters on customer service or customer quality but also for a wide range of other purposes such as strategic planning, research and development, creativity and innovation, and, in this case, learning. Under TQM, synergogy is the preferred learning mode.

- The two alternative systems to synergogy are pedagogy and androgogy.

- *Pedagogy* (*ped* means child and *gogy* means teaching) is the authoritarian system we first encounter as children. An authority figure stands in front of us and tells us what's what. The term *trainer,* which is widely used in industry, still conveys the authoritarian idea that someone, the trainer, is going to make it clear and certain to someone else, the learner, what's what.

- In *androgogy* (adult learning), which is the most common model used in large organizations, the instructor is still in charge but acts more as a facilitator.

- Mouton and Blake describe the four ways in which synergogy differs from the other two models:

1. It replaces authority figures with learning designs and instruments managed by a learning administrator;

2. It enables learners to become proactive participants who exercise responsibility for their own learning;

3. It applies the concept of synergy—the learning gain that results from teamwork exceeds the gain made by individual learning alone;

4. The teamwork atmosphere provides motivation for learning.

TEAMWORK

- TQM brings about an increase in the spirit of teamwork among the members of the enterprise, the company and its suppliers, and the company and its customers.

- This spirit of teamwork and a habit of mutual support and assistance is brought about by TQM's emphasis on human as well as financial values.

- Teamwork is also fostered in TQM companies by the creation of a climate of openness, trust, and confidence.

- It is reinforced by such common TQM practices as multifunctional and multilevel teams, quality celebrations, and the study and practice by all concerned of many basic management methods.

- The sense of sharing in a common cause also stimulates teamwork.

- The heightened teamwork and cooperation greatly adds to the speed and efficiency with which things are done, problems solved, and innovative ideas put into operation.

TECHNOLOGY MANAGEMENT

- TQM firms—having a high quality of strategizing at the top management level—regard modern technologies as resources that can make the firm more powerful, enable it to produce and deliver new and superior products and services, and permit it to serve markets and customers more effectively.

- Along with good people, good technology ranks high among the list of factors that make a firm more globally competitive.

- To rank as a quality company means to rank high in technology management. Technology management is emerging as a distinct art and science in its own right in the same sense as financial management, marketing management, or manufacturing management are. Quality in technology is therefore a prerequisite for having quality in products and in customer service.

- Some firms have vice presidents of T. M. whose function includes helping the firm make strategic use of every technology possible and desirable, in every phase of the business, for every purpose of the business, and in ways that are as powerful and effective as possible.

- Several universities now offer special programs leading to graduate degrees in Technology Management. Technology management is a growing field of scholarly research.

- The larger management consulting firms now contain important divisions devoted specifically to helping their clients to manage technology both strategically and operationally.

- In all modern firms, strategic technology management necessarily means the astute use of information technologies, ranging through computers, teleconferencing, faxes, satellites, cellular phones, video phones, multimedia, robotics, automation, expert systems, artificial intelligence, virtual reality, and more to come.

- But in most firms strategic technology management also includes one or more other equally important technologies. The strategic significance of these other technologies can also be immense.

- For example, McDonald's, which has always boasted a very sophisticated R&D department, won a strategic advantage over its competitors when it developed a technology and an oven for producing pizzas in a fraction of the conventional time.

- Again, ecologically benign automobiles, powered by hydrogen extracted from lake water, or by electricity generated through the electrolysis of aluminum, will offer their developers some strategic marketing advantages. (In the aluminum-powered car of the future, if the body is also made from aluminum and the car runs out of fuel, some wag has suggested it will merely mean having to tear off a fender.)

- Biotechnology is opening up whole new industries such as prosthetics and transforming others such as agriculture. Gene splicing is resulting in new crops and new animals. Genetic engineering is leading to the elimination or treatment of an ever-lengthening list of diseases and disorders. Biotechnology may have human, social, and economic impacts even greater than transportation technology, materials, or information technology all added together.

- In TQM firms, technology has a human face. Everyone is given maximum training and support in the use of new technologies, and participates in the selection and/or design of technologies.

- In the TQM view, people and machines work in a symbiotic relationship in which machines complement the work of humans and humans complement the work of machines.

- This human-machine relationship is referred to by some as a "sociotechnical system." It is sometimes described—if properly designed—as a "high-performance work system." Xerox calls their human-machine systems "productive work communities."

- Not only have computers and computer networks already made it easier to flatten organizations structures and reduce the number of levels in the hierarchy, but they are affecting the social and human climate of the workplace as well. As Francis Bacon put it centuries ago, knowledge is power. By making available to everyone the knowledge and information that used to be restricted to higher-ups, everyone becomes more equal. Network conversations between people at different levels in the hierarchy then become commonplace. What you have to say is more important than who you are. The computer network thus creates a social climate that corresponds effectively with the spirit of TQM, its use of team problem-solving processes, and its need to find more ways to empower employees.

THREE-DIMENSIONAL MANAGERS

- Three-dimensional managers are the type of managers that are found in the TQM company. They function not only as managers in the classical sense, but also as leaders and as innovators/entrepreneurs.

- As classical managers, they help their teams to plan, organize, coordinate, measure, and control.

- As leaders they envision, imagine, foresee, inspire, teach, and excite. They are trailblazers.

- As innovators/entrepreneurs they seize on opportunity, master change, and bring forward all those new things that have the marvelous power to create and transform.

TIME-BASED MANAGEMENT

- Time-based management, an important aspect of TQM, focuses on time as it affects the firm's ability to keep up with and move ahead of the competition, as it affects the costs of production and delivery, and as it affects customer service and satisfaction.

- Time has a special meaning in a world where things are already moving fast, and where the speed increases with every passing day. Jonathan C. Crane, a senior vice president of MCI Telecommunications, put it this way: *"Speed of response has joined accuracy, craftsmanship, creativity, resourcefulness, and other traditional measures of quality. And in many cases, timing ranks first."*

- Time is the dimension in which change takes place, and time flies. Firms have to develop and market new products constantly and must be able to design and develop them in the shortest possible elapsed time; if they don't, their competitors will.

- Moreover, as Ben Franklin put it long ago, *"Time is money."* To a company, human time is an economic resource that has to be paid for and can be bought and sold. The cost of making and delivering products or services is largely the cost of the time it takes people to do so, and people are paid for their time by the hour, day, month, or year. A large portion of the corporate budget is heavily allocated to purchasing human time in the form of annual, weekly, daily, or hourly wages and salaries. This purchased pool of human time must be strategically deployed and efficiently employed in ways that are cost-effective. TQM firms search endlessly for ways of doing things that take as little of the time of the people who do them as possible. The effective and efficient management of the corporate time resource is one of the major skills of the TQM executive.

- The management of customer time ranks equal in importance. Customers need or want things fast—immediate delivery—and want products or services that give them what they want with the minimum waste of their time. TQM firms use process improvement and process re-engineering to reduce time intervals and speed things up.

- Time-based management is particularly sensitive to the simple equation that to the human being time is the very essence of existence. No one ever expressed this idea better than Benjamin Franklin did when he said *"Dost thou love life? Then do not squander time; for that's the stuff life is made of."*

- Consumers want the time they spend buying to be extra-pleasant and enjoyable. They certainly don't want the seller to give them a bad time! People hate waiting in line, or spending time in unpleasant surroundings, or spending time uncomfortably, or spending time being bored.

- Consumer-focused companies go through hoops in order to make every minute spent with them an enjoyable minute. Ten minutes spent waiting in a line feels ten times as long as ten minutes doing enjoyable things—ten minutes chatting with a friend or watching a good movie. The Toronto Dominion Bank, in 1981 arguably the first bank in the world to get into quality management, pays five dollars to any customer who waits in line for more than five minutes. Some banks provide television programs for customers to watch while they wait in line. Some provide pleasant music and an elegant decor.

- Many products, such as dishwashers, frozen meals, and numerous others, were created simply to save people from spending time doing things they either don't have time to do or don't like doing. The market for time-saving and time-enhancing products and services is immense and growing.

- In the production domain, time-based management includes such methodologies as just-in-time manufacturing, in which products are manufactured when the customer needs them rather than beforehand.

- Furthermore, the TQM company's heightened consciousness of the social, human, and economic importance of time has led to an increase in the use of such old and new employee relations policies and practices as rest breaks, happy hours, flexible hours, job sharing, work-sharing, shortened work-weeks, compassionate leave, sabbatical leave, variable retirement ages, and so on.

- The management of time also includes developing personal skill in reducing and eliminating routine activities that are not worth the time and replacing them with valuable, high-payoff, creative activities that are maximally rewarding. Examples of low payoff are doing things that others could do for you, reading useless reports, or supervising people too closely. Examples of high-payoff uses of time are calisthenics, learning, human relationships, creative thinking, planning, communicating, and motivating. The distinction between high-payoff time and low-payoff time is a key concept in time-based management.

TOTAL INVOLVEMENT

- TQM deeply involves all employees, on a daily basis, in striving to increase the satisfactions, and meet the expectations of their internal and/or external customers through delivering better products and services.

- In addition, all employees are deeply involved in examining and improving the processes through which services or products are produced and delivered.

- In these and other ways, TQM employees are fully involved in the quest for quality. No longer are quality assurance and quality control people the only ones seriously involved, as once was the case. Involvement now embraces everyone in the organization; there are no exceptions, because everyone, in every department, is striving to improve his or her own quality as well as trying to help associates improve theirs.

- Moreover, the TQM company involves its customers and suppliers in the whole process.

- The CEO, in particular, could be said to be the one person most involved through his or her constant effort to inspire, lead, and support the whole quality effort. Quality is one key priority that TQM CEOs and their immediate reports demonstrate a constant concern for. Their concern is visible to the whole organization. Top management and grassroots involvement are equally critical to quality performance. If the CEO isn't trying to improve himself or herself and his or her work, the employees won't try either.

TOTAL QUALITY MANAGEMENT

- The word "total" was first introduced into the quality management field by Dr. A. V. Feigenbaum. He used it in his phrase "total quality control" to make the point that the quality of everything in the business, not only of products and services, is of importance. As quality came to be seen as something that had to be created as well as controlled, and as it was seen to include processes as well as products, the phrase "total quality management" was substituted.

- The implications of the word *total* are profound. It applies to the quality of the strategic thinking exhibited by executives, to the quality of the firm's ethics, to the quality of training, to the quality of technology management, to the quality of communications, in short, to the quality of everything. It is only when the full meaning of the word *total* is appreciated that a firm can truly said to be committed to the ideal of TQM.

- For a firm to achieve its full potential, nothing in the firm can remain untouched by TQM's philosophy of excellence in all things.

TRAINING IN TQM

- Can you believe it? Complete training in TQM can take as long as two years of full-time courses as is the case at the American River Community College in Sacramento, California. The college now has 450 students registered in a two-year TQM degree program, which was established in 1986.

- However, most training is provided by in-house consultants or by specialized consulting firms and organizations who provide public seminars and in-house courses.

- Non-profit organizations and associations are big providers. The American Productivity & Quality Center, to take one example, has a battery of over 20 different quality and productivity courses provided in different cities, throughout the year. The Center for Quality Management leads senior executives through two years of intense training, implementation, and shared learning exercises.

- Many universities and community colleges provide short one-day to one-week orientation courses on TQM. Some provide a series of different courses on the different parts of TQM.

TRANSFORMATIVE CHANGE

- In transformation the character of a thing or a condition is altered from one form to another wholly unique form. Some examples:

1. The change that takes place when water turns to ice.

2. The change that takes place when love turns to hate.

3. The change that takes place when a person gets very drunk.

4. The change that takes place at puberty.

5. The change that takes place when a person enters prison.

6. The change that takes place when an agricultural economy becomes a manufacturing economy.

7. The USSR's change from communism to free enterprise.

8. The change that has taken place in GE under the transformative leadership of Jack Welch.

9. The change that took place at Ford under the transformative leadership of Donald Petersen.

10. The change that takes place when participative management replaces the command and control style.

11. The change that takes place when a company becomes service-driven rather than profit-driven.

12. The change that takes place when a company makes quality rather than size a measure of its excellence.

- Success in moving into TQM depends on realizing in advance that TQM is not a process of improving the old concepts of business and management but of replacing them with new ones that are different in character. The result will be a transformed company.

- Without a readiness to see TQM as a transformation rather than as a nice new add-on, as frosting on the cake, not much will be accomplished. Little will result.

- When a company does go TQM in the full and complete sense, it will engage in a process of transformation. Its previous form and character will alter in every single respect. The transformed company will then bear little resemblance to the company it had previously been. The performance of the transformed firm will reach levels of quality and excellence that would have been previously inconceivable.

- The ancient dream of changing lead into gold will have been accomplished. An exaggeration? Not if you look at the companies where it has happened.

UNLEARNING

- If a thin wall with a hole in it is placed in the middle of a goldfish tank, the goldfish will learn to swim to the hole to get to food on the other side. After the wall is removed, the goldfish will continue to swim to where the hole used to be whenever it has to cross the tank. It never unlearns its old ways. (Japan Human Relations Association, 1988, p. 38)

- Humans can have the same problem. It is therefore increasingly recognized that the first step in learning is often to "unlearn" the old answers of the past. Unlearning is many times more difficult than learning. Learning is relatively easy. It's what humans are best at.

- TQM requires a great deal of unlearning of past business and management habits and practices, some of which may have been matters of deep belief and conviction. This is one reason why it takes years for an organization to fully make the shift to a fully functioning TQM mode.

VALUES

- Values are the fundamental criteria that people, societies, and organizations use in deciding what is most important to them.

- For example, to some people science is considered more important than art, and to others the reverse is true. To some people, good character is more important than beauty and good grooming, and to others it is not. It's easy to extend this list of value differences almost endlessly.

- Some societies value art more than science, and others the reverse. In some firms, achieving maximum profitability is more important than achieving sales volume and size while others prefer bigness over profitability. In some cultures (for example, Japan) politeness is more important than candor, and in others (for example, the U.S.) the reverse is true. Some have an in-between position (for example, Canada).

- Values are enormously significant in business life. Differences in values account for much of the differences that will be found between one company and another. Values will govern or influence a company's choice of goals, its priorities, and even its strategies. For example, some companies value toughness to the point of abrasion while others value diplomacy and friendliness in business dealings. In some companies, the marketing function is more highly valued than manufacturing, and in others the opposite is true. Some companies value risk-taking while others value prudence more. Some corporate cultures value compliance and cooperation more than assertiveness and individuality, and others vice-versa.

- TQM organizations tend to share a number of values in common. Among the things that TQM organizations commonly value are human dignity, integrity, social responsibilities, stakeholders rights, customer satisfaction, teams and teamwork, education and training, employee empowerment, continuous improvement, sound business ethics, honest communication, analytical and creative thinking, strategy and planning, value for money, advanced technology, change and innovation, and of course profitability. Many companies place a high premium on some of these individual values but what characterizes the TQM companies is that they subscribe to most of them, and even all of them.

- Even so differences in values will cause one company's particular spin on TQM to be quite different from any others. These differences are as interesting as any of the similarities. TQM company A is a bear on tightly integrated supplier relations and a bit less strong on customer relations, but in TQM company B, the reverse is true. And so the differences may go, right across the whole spectrum. One thing that TQM will never produce is total uniformity.

VALUE-ADDED

- Value gets added to materials, products, or services whenever they are changed, improved, moved, or transformed in a way that makes them more useful, satisfying, or desirable to the purchaser or the consumer.

- When raw lumber is cut, then nailed into a garden shed, and the shed is made easily available from a local retail outlet, it has much more value than the original lumber and nails. At each step, value has been added. Going back farther in the value-adding process, the lumber was once a log and that log had been given added value by being cut and planed into lumber. The nails were once iron ore, which acquired more value after it had been smelted, extruded as wire, cut into nail length, and given a head. Going a step ahead in the value-adding process, if the vendor delivers the shed right to your garden, the vendor has added still more value to what has been done for you.

- When clerical workers become computer literate they make themselves more valuable in the eyes of prospective employers. The result may be jobs at higher pay. If some take another step and add further value to themselves by developing desktop publishing skills or computer graphics expertise, the market may pay them even more.

- The sequence of processes through which a business takes raw inputs and moves them stage by stage to the final form of the ultimately delivered product or service is referred to as the "value-added chain."

- The value-added chain includes the supplier relationships at the beginning of the process and may extend even past the point of purchase in follow-up services and maintenance programs.

VISION

- A vision is the image that a person or an organization has of what it wants to become and what it wants to achieve, expressed in a form that is concrete and pictorial enough that when communicated it forms an equally vivid image in the listener's mind.

- Burt Nanus of the University of California says that a vision should offer a realistic, credible, attractive future for your organization.

- My colleague Bill Christopher puts it this way:

Vision sets a direction for the future. It says for everyone in the company, "This is the road we will follow in all that we do, to create a successful future."

- Organizations that have no true sense of mission and purpose, that are not values-driven, that are not outward-looking and future-focused, that are not imaginative, will not generally be able to construct a vision of their future.

VOCABULARY

- The vocabulary of TQM is very similar in the U.S., Canada, Mexico, and the various countries of Europe, and among industries and companies, largely because much of the same body of ideas is shared.

- At the same time, there are definite differences in viewpoint and emphasis and these give rise to some differences in vocabulary. Besides, the vocabulary constantly calls for new words as our experience with TQM unfolds and new perspectives emerge. This year's TQM is never last year's TQM, but something more and better. The TQM described in this book is a TQM that far outstrips in scope and depth what was being called TQM just a couple of years ago.

- In addition, TQM is often called by different names, depending on the preference of the company. For example, CN railroad uses the term "Quality of Work" to cover their extremely broad-reaching approach, which is essentially identical to what is presented in this handbook. The French firm Thompson Consumer Electronics calls it the "Quality Leadership Process." General Motors calls theirs the "General Motors Quality Network."

- Words and phrases are tricky things. The fact that an organization has a "Vice President of Quality" or a "Manager of Quality" does not necessarily mean that company embraces or practices the philosophy of TQM. In most cases, it will not. It will often merely mean they want to make a strong attempt to achieve improvement in products and services and in nothing else, and by using orthodox means. There is no assumption of a fundamental change in corporate culture. There is no fundamental new thinking. In that case, experience indicates that their success will be modest at best.

WALKING THE TALK

- "Walking the talk" is a phrase frequently repeated in TQM companies as a reminder that one has to be constantly on guard against the pitfalls of having much talk and little action or, worse, of talking one way and acting another.

- It is reminiscent of the remark:

  What you do speaks so loudly that I cannot hear what you say.

- Similar to the sentiment expressed 600 years before Christ by Siddhartha Gautama:

  A man who talks much of his teaching but does not practice it himself is like a cattleman counting another man's cattle.

  Like beautiful flowers of color, but without scent, are the well-chosen words of the man who does not act accordingly.

WASTE

- One measure of the quality of management is its ability to conduct business in an economical manner, getting the most value from the available resources.

- Using this criterion of economy, it follows that the waste and squandering of the firm's resources of materials, space, equipment, time, or human talent is to be avoided.

- My own surveys of management groups have revealed that managers on the average believe that most of the firms they have been associated with waste 40 to 60 percent of the available physical, financial, and human resources, particularly human time.

- What this level of waste means is that most firms can substantially improve their profits and their competitive position simply by tracking down and eliminating or reducing it.

- In the poor quality firm, waste is visible everywhere; in a TQM firm there is a constant search for waste that can be eliminated. In today's world of scarce resources and environmental pollution, reasonable frugality in the use of resources has come to be regarded as an ethical imperative as well as a competitive necessity, and the socially responsible firm commits itself therefore to the goal of waste minimization and reduction.

WISDOM

Where is the wisdom we have lost in knowledge?
Where is the knowledge we have lost in information?
     T. S. ELIOT

- Wisdom is the ability to know what is important and what is unimportant, what is right and what is wrong; to be able to foresee the consequences of actions; and to distinguish between what is going to work and produce benefits, and what will be counterproductive.

- Wisdom is not the same as knowledge. It's common to see knowledgeable managers doing foolish things that will make situations worse. Wisdom is found more often in people who understand things than it is in people who merely know a lot. Wisdom is to the manager what knowledge is to the knowledge worker, namely his or her stock in trade.

- TQM won't work unless those who implement it understand that it is a long-term commitment aimed at transforming the enterprise. They must understand that it is based on an ethic of genuine—unfaked—interest in the customer and the employee. They must understand that it means trusting others, being open to others, and being willing to listen to them.

- TQM has to be understood not merely as a set of observable methods (such as quality teams, statistical process control, customer surveys, etc.) but as a new way of thinking and feeling and understanding what business can be all about.

- Managers wise enough to understand what TQM really is will also have the wisdom to introduce it in the right way, instead of violating its nature and ignoring its true meaning.

ZEALOTS

- Zealots in early Judaism were those who showed zeal (religious fanaticism) on behalf of the law.

- Nowadays, the term *zealot* is generally used to describe anyone who is fanatical about anything, including TQM.

- For most people, fanatics can be pretty hard to take and are seen as lacking a sense of proportion and, worse still, a sense of humor.

- Still, it does take a bit of zeal to make TQM work.

ZERO BASED BUDGETING

- Zero based budgeting is a form of forward-looking rather than backward-looking budgetary thinking.

- In ZBB, budgets are prepared with no respect for the sanctity of the previous year's expenditures. They are not based on what last year's budget was, neither in total nor for particular items. Instead, the idea is to start from scratch, from zero.

- In ZBB, the objectives for the next year and the next five or more years are formulated, and then the staffing, equipment, plans, and programs to achieve them are delineated. Following this, the expenditures needed to achieve these objectives are calculated.

- Instead of extending the past into the future, the idea is to extend the future backwards to the present. Start with where you want to end up, figure out what it will cost you to get there, and that will be your budget. That's how the future is invented.

- Harold Geneen, the former president of ITT, constantly reminded his managers that management is the opposite of reading:

  You read a book from the beginning to the end. You run a business the opposite way. You start with the end, then you do everything you must to reach it.

- Performing the Geneen trick is one of the secrets of personal and business success. It's a skill that can be learned. But first one has to realize that the skill exists and that it is necessary.

- Dr. Charles E. Smith, an international management consultant based in McLean, Virginia, calls the process of working your mind backward from the future the "Merlin Factor," in honor of Merlin the Magician in King Arthur's Court. Merlin was born with the remarkable ability to see the past, present, and future all in a single glance. It made it easy for him to tell King Arthur what had to be done next in order to achieve success. If he were alive today, Merlin would be an advocate of ZBB.

- Zero based budgeting is logically consistent both with activity based accounting and with management by objectives. Ideally, a firm operating in the TQM mode will aim for the principle of zero based budgeting.

- It is easy to apply ZBB to a new project such as an R&D project or an advertising program but difficult to apply it to an ongoing operation that already exists. Even then, it is useful to picture the operation at zero, and then visualize what expenditures would really have to be made. The exercise will often reveal new possibilities for more cost-effective ways to proceed in the present. The task is to change what needs to be changed and create what needs to be created to get to the goal. ZBB is both a state of mind and a method.

ZERO DEFECTS

- A program developed by Philip B. Crosby, originally for quality management of the Pershing missile project at Martin Marietta Corp.

- The term *zero defects* proposes as a quality management goal the absolute absence of any defects.

- Crosby proposes that zero defects should be a goal, not only for *some* kinds of work such as missile building or brain surgery, but for *all* work.

- Zero defects is an expression of the philosophy of perfectionism, the belief that humanity should strive for the perfection of all things; the idea runs as a continuous current through much of human history.

- Perfectionism is not a philosophy that all students of quality management subscribe to or endorse as always desirable, necessary, or practical.

- This edition, while hoping to be more useful than the first, still has defects and deficiencies. The next edition will be better. We're committed to continuous improvement. And maybe to a quantum leap or two.

ZEROING IN

- All we really need to know to do TQM is that the purpose of any business is to produce customer satisfaction. Everything else will flow from that principle, logically and inexorably.

- Any alternative construction will lead away from quality. The logic for that conclusion is equally infallible. And the evidence is everywhere.

Bibliography

Akao, Yoji. *Hoshin Kanri: Policy Deployment for Successful TQM.* Portland, Or. : Productivity Press, 1991.

Akao, Yoji. *Quality Function Deployment.* Portland, Or.: Productivity Press, 1991.

Albrecht, Karl. *The Only Thing that Matters: Bringing the Power of the Customer into the Center of Your Business.* New York: Harper Collins, 1992.

American Productivity & Quality Center. *The Benchmarking Management Guide.* Portland, Or. : Productivity Press, 1993.

Aubrey, Charles A., II. *Quality Management in Financial Services.* Wheaton, Ill.: Hitchcock, 1992.

Barrett, Derm, "Driving Quality and Productivity Improvement Ahead Through Idea Generation," chap. 2-7.1 in *Handbook for Productivity Measurement and Improvement,* William F. Christopher and Carl Thor, ed., Portland, Or.: Productivity Press, 1993.

Berry, Len, Parsu Parasuraman, and Valerie Zeithaml. "A Conceptual Model of Service Quality and Its Implications for Future Research," *Journal of Marketing,* Fall 1985: 41-50.

Christopher, William F. , and Carl G. Thor. *Handbook for Productivity Measurement and Improvement.* Portland, Or. : Productivity Press, 1993.

de Bono, Edward. *Lateral Thinking: Creativity Step by Step*. New York: Harper Collins, 1973.

GOAL/QPC. *The Memory Jogger.* Methuen, Mass.: GOAL/QPC, 1988.

Japan Human Relations Association, ed. *The Idea Book.* Portland, Or. : Productivity Press, 1988.

Johnson, H. Thomas, and Robert F. Kaplan. *Relevance Lost: The Rise and Fall of Management Accounting.* Cambridge: Harvard Business School Press, 1986.

Kotler, Philip. *Marketing Management.* Englewood Cliffs, N.J.: Prentice-Hall, 1984.

Main, Jeremy. "How to Win the Baldrige Award," *Fortune,* April 23, 1990.

Mangan, Katherine S. "TQM: Colleges Embrace the Concept of 'Total Quality Management,'" *The Chronicle of Higher Education,* August 12, 1992.

May, Rollo. *The Courage to Create.* New York: Bantam, 1984.

Michael, Donald N. *The Future Society.* Hawthorne, N.Y.: Aldine de Gruyter, 1970.

Moore, Kay. "University of Maryland: 'TQM' in Action," *The Quality Observer,* July 1992.

Morgan, Gareth. *Imaginization: The Art of Creative Management.* Sage, 1993.

Mouton, Jane, and Robert Blake. *Synergogy: A New Strategy for Education, Training, and Development.* San Francisco: Jossey-Bass, 1984.

Odiorne, George. *The Human Side of Management.* New York: Free Press, 1987.

Osborne, Alex. *Applied Imagination,* 3d ed. New York: Scribner, 1963.

Pedler, Mike, John Burgoyne, and Tom Boydell. *The Learning Company.* London: McGraw-Hill, 1991.

Potts, Mark, and Peter Behr. *The Leading Edge.* New York: McGraw-Hill, 1987.

Prince, George. *The Practice of Creativity: A Manual for Dynamic Groups.* New York: Harper & Row, 1970.

Stewart, Thomas A. "Reengineering: The Hot New Management Tool," *Fortune,* August 23, 1993, p. 42.

Tenner, Arthur R. , and Irving J. DeToro. *Total Quality Management.* Reading, Mass. : Addison-Wesley, 1992.

Thomas, Noel G. "Total Quality Management (TQM) Hinges on Management's Commitment," *Technology Source* 5, no. 1:3 (1992).

Toffler, Alvin. *Future Shock.* New York: Bantam, 1971.

Watson, Thomas J. *A Business and Its Beliefs: The Ideas That Helped Build IBM.* New York: McGraw-Hill, 1963.

Wiener, Norbert. *Cybernetics: Communication and Control in Man and Machine.* New York: John Wiley & Sons, 1948.

About the Author

Derm Barrett specializes internationally in the strategic management of quality, change, creativity, and innovation, working hands-on with clients in the United States, Canada, Europe, and South America. He is president of Toronto-based Management Concepts Limited, is a member of The Management Innovations Group in Stamford, Connecticut, and is the North American representative of Grupo Norma of Madrid, Spain.

Dr. Barrett has held executive positions with Alcan and CN Railways. Prior to organizing Management Concepts Limited some years ago, he had been successively associate director of the Banff School of Advanced Management, chairman of the Executive Development Program at Queen's, and founding director of the Division of Executive Development at York University in Toronto. He holds a B. Sc. in psychology from McGill and a Ph. D. in industrial economics from MIT.

BOOKS FROM PRODUCTIVITY PRESS

Productivity Press publishes and distributes materials on continuous improvement in productivity, quality, and the creative involvement of all employees. Many of our products are direct source materials from Japan that have been translated into English for the first time and are available exclusively from Productivity. Supplemental products and services include membership groups, conferences, seminars, in-house training and consulting, audio-visual training programs, and industrial study missions. Call toll-free 1-800-394-6868 for our free catalog.

A New American TQM
Four Practical Revolutions in Management
Shoji Shiba, Alan Graham, and David Walden

For TQM to succeed in America, you need to create an American-style "learning organization" with the full commitment and understanding of senior managers and executives. Written expressly for this audience, *A New American TQM* offers a comprehensive and detailed explanation of TQM and how to implement it, based on courses taught at MIT's Sloan School of Management and the Center for Quality Management, a consortium of American hi-tech companies. Full of case studies and amply illustrated, the book examines major quality tools and how they are being used by the most progressive American companies today.
ISBN 1-56327-032-3 / 606 pages / $49.95 / Order NATQM-B147

Companywide Quality Management
Alberto Galgano

Companywide quality management (CWQM) leads to dramatic changes in management values and priorities, company culture, management of company operations, management and decision-making processes, techniques and methods used by employees, and more. Much has been written on this subject, but Galgano—a leading European consultant who studied with leaders of the Japanese quality movement—offers hands-on, stage-front knowledge of the monumental changes CWQC can bring.
ISBN 1-56327-038-2 / 480 pages / $45.00 / Order CWQM-B147

Achieving Total Quality Management
A Program for Action
Michel Perigord

This is an outstanding book on total quality management (TQM) — a compact guide to the concepts, methods, and techniques involved in achieving total quality. It shows you how to make TQM a companywide strategy, not just in technical areas, but in marketing and administration as well. Major methods and tools for total quality are spelled out and implementation strategies are reviewed.
ISBN 0-915299-60-7 / 392 pages / $49.95 / Order ACHTQM-B147

Productivity Press, Inc. Dept. BK, P.O. Box 13390, Portland, OR 97213-0390
Telephone: 1-800-394-6868 Fax: 1-800-394-6286

Hoshin Kanri
Policy Deployment for Successful TQM
Yoji Akao (ed.)

Hoshin kanri, the Japanese term for policy deployment, is an approach to strategic planning and quality improvement that has become a pillar of Total Quality Management (TQM) for a growing number of U.S. firms. This book is a compilation of examples of policy deployment that demonstrates how company vision is converted into individual responsibility. It includes practical guidelines, 150 charts and diagrams, and five case studies that illustrate the procedures of *hoshin kanri.* The six steps to advanced process planning are reviewed and include a five-year vision, one-year plan, deployment to departments, execution, monthly audit, and annual audit.
ISBN 0-915299-57-7 / 241 pages / $65.00 / Order HOSHIN-B147

Management for Quality Improvement
The 7 New QC Tools
Shigeru Mizuno, ed.

Building on the traditional seven QC tools, these tools were developed specifically for managers. They help in planning, troubleshooting, and communicating with maximum effectiveness at every stage of a quality improvement program and are certain to advance quality improvement efforts for anyone involved in project management, quality assurance, MIS, or TQC.
ISBN 0-915299-29-1 / 323 pages / $65.00 / Order 7QC-B147

The New Standardization
Keystone of Continuous Improvement in Manufacturing
Shigehiro Nakamura

In an era of continuous improvement and ISO 9000, quality is not an option but a requirement, and you can't set or meet criteria for quality without standardization. Standardization lets you share information about the best ways to do things so that they will be done that way consistently. This book shows how to make standardization a living system of just-in-time information that delivers exactly the information that's needed, exactly when it is needed, and exactly where it is needed. It's the only way to sustain the results of your improvement efforts in every area of your company.
ISBN 1-56327-039-0 / 286 pages / $75.00 / Order STAND-B147

The Benchmarking Management Guide
American Productivity & Quality Center

If you're planning, organizing, or actually undertaking a benchmarking program, you need the most authoritative source of information to help you get started and to manage the process all the way through. Written expressly for managers of benchmarking projects by the APQC's renowned International Benchmarking Clearinghouse, this guide provides exclusive information from members who have already paved the way. It includes information on training courses and ways to apply Baldrige, Deming, and ISO 9000 criteria for internal assessment, and has a complete bibliography of benchmarking literature.
ISBN 1-56327-045-5 / 260 pages / $39.95 / Order BMG-B147

Productivity Press, Inc. Dept. BK, P.O. Box 13390, Portland, OR 97213-0390
Telephone: 1-800-394-6868 Fax: 1-800-394-6286

The Benchmarking Workbook
Adapting Best Practices for Performance Improvement
Gregory H. Watson

Managers today need benchmarking to anticipate trends and maintain competitive advantage. This practical workbook shows you how to do your own benchmarking study. Watson's discussion includes a case study that takes you through each step of the benchmarking process, raises thought-provoking questions, and provides examples of how to use forms for a benchmarking study.
ISBN 1-56327-033-1 / 169 pages / $29.95 / Order BENCHW-B147

TQM for Technical Groups
Total Quality Principles for Product Development
Kiyoshi Uchimaru, Susumu Okamoto, and Bunteru Kurahara

Achieving total quality in product design and development is a daunting but essential goal for technical personnel. This unprecedented and highly practical book was written especially for technical groups working to achieve total quality in product development. Originally published by JUSE, the Union of Japanese Scientists and Engineers, the book includes an important case study of NEC IC Microcomputer Systems, winner of the Deming Prize. A separate section of the book addresses all the changes required in corporate management to institute TQM at the product design level. Step-by-step instructions, with specific examples of each, show you how to plan, implement, and sustain an effective TQM program.
ISBN 1-56327-005-6 / 258 pages / $60.00 / Order TQMTG-B147

TO ORDER: Write, phone, or fax Productivity Press, Dept. BK, 541 NE 20th Ave., Portland, OR 97232, phone 1-800-394-6868, fax 1-800-394-6286. Send check or charge to your credit card (American Express, Visa, MasterCard accepted).

U.S. ORDERS: Add $5 shipping for first book, $2 each additional for UPS surface delivery. We offer attractive quantity discounts for bulk purchases of individual titles; call for more information.

INTERNATIONAL ORDERS: Write, phone, or fax for quote and indicate shipping method desired. For international callers, telephone number is 503-235-0600 and fax number is 503-235-0909. Prepayment in U.S. dollars must accompany your order (checks must be drawn on U.S. banks). When quote is returned with payment, your order will be shipped promptly by the method requested.

NOTE: Prices are in U.S. dollars and are subject to change without notice.

Productivity Press, Inc. Dept. BK, P.O. Box 13390, Portland, OR 97213-0390
Telephone: 1-800-394-6868 Fax: 1-800-394-6286